Exeter Maritime Studies · Number Six

Edited by Stephen Fisher

INNOVATION
IN SHIPPING AND TRADE

ref 11/Unit 635

£5.99

EXETER MARITIME STUDIES

General Editor: Stephen Fisher

Innovation in Shipping and Trade
First published 1989 by the
University of Exeter

© 1989 Department of Economic and Social History
University of Exeter
ISBN 0 85989 327 8

University of Exeter Press
Reed Hall
Streatham Drive
Exeter, Devon, EX4 4QR

Typeset by Nota Bene with Postscript
at the University of Exeter

Printed and Bound in Great Britain
by Short Run Press Ltd, Exeter

To Basil Greenhill and Joyce Youings
for introducing me to
new scholarly maritime interests,
and proving such estimable collaborators
in the New Maritime History of Devon project.
(*The ed.*)

ACKNOWLEDGMENTS

The editor of this collection wishes to express his gratitude to Alessandra Saxton and Loveday Metcalfe for their efficient wordprocessing, Ray Burnley and Rebecca Tucker of the Social Studies Data Processing Unit for expert technical help, and James Gould of the University's Graphic Design Unit for kindly designing the book's covers and preparing the illustrations for the printer. As ever, Barbara Mennell of the University Press gave good advice and support. Special thanks are also owed to the two benefactors (who wish to remain anonymous) who supported the publication of this volume. Finally, the members of the Dartington conference wish to reiterate their appreciation of the work of the Warden and staff of the Devon Centre, Dartington Hall in helping to make our meetings so pleasurable.

CONTENTS

List of Illustrations

Illustrations 1,3,4 and 5 are reproduced by kind permission of the National Maritime Museum, Greenwich.

INTRODUCTION

This volume offers a further collection of research papers presented (or in one case about to be presented) at the annual Dartington maritime history conference organised by the Department of Economic and Social History of Exeter University. The collection illustrates the declared aim of broadening the conference's range of interests:[1] that is, to cover national and international maritime-related historical issues, while not forgetting the West Country maritime research out of which this conference sprang.

With one exception the papers (the exception is David Williams' excellent advocacy of the picture postcard as a source for maritime historical research) bear on the broad theme of innovation in shipping and trade. Innovation in maritime-related affairs, as in other areas of economy or society, is what marks the lively and creative from the static or stagnant. The innovations dealt with, technological or business, are for the most part British, one of the early seventeenth century but in the main relating to that outstanding age of the British as innovators, the later eighteenth and first half of the nineteenth centuries. In contrast, Stephanie Jones' contribution throws light on the waning of this age in Britain, in her study of conservative management in the shipping group, P & O, in the 1920s.

The first paper though, by Keith Hamilton-Smith and Ewan Corlett, is concerned with a profound shipping innovation in the world of antiquity, the ancient Athenian trireme, or *trieres* as the Greeks called it. This vessel has, of course, been the subject of much recent investigation and debate, leading to the reconstruction and sailing trials of a replica vessel off Poros in the Aegean. Oared warships, of which the *trieres*, a vessel driven by three banks of oars, is the most famous, lie as Morrison and Coates put it, 'at the heart of the Greek, Hellenistic and Roman story as it unfolds from Homer to Constantine'. In their view the vessel has a twofold importance; first, because its design was basic to the development of all subsequent oared warships in the classical world. And second, because it had so significant a role in preserving the political and economic conditions necessary for the flowering of Athenian civilisation. This was crucially so at the battle of Salamis in 480 B.C. when the fleet of *trieres* built shortly before and specifically designed by Themistocles 'for speed and quick turning', according to Plutarch, enabled the Greeks to repel the second Persian invasion.[2]

Our authors, drawing on their professional expertise as ship's architects and engineers, are concerned to analyse further the basic technical parameters of a *trieres*. They offer some most interesting findings, and put forward, in particular, the hypotheses that the *trieres* may well have been fitted with a primitive form of

1

sliding seat, and that the main offensive weapon, the ram – the *trieres* was a form of projectile whose purpose was to ram and so disable or sink an enemy – would not, indeed could not, have been aligned parallel to the keel or baseline. In their judgement the historically-quoted performances of the *trieres* were indeed possible. Their paper offers a lucid technical analysis of a dramatic ship design, fascinating to a mere modern historian. (One might add too that to one who has been privileged to have sailed the 'wine-dark seas' off Poros and to have seen the Salamis channel, the paper has a special resonance).

A much later major innovation in mankind's use of ships, also with profound social and economic consequences, was the nineteenth-century introduction of steam power – the harnessing of the 'benignant power of steam' in Andrew Ure's phase. It is difficult to exaggerate the impact over time of the steam engine, whether on land or sea, symbolising as it does the Industrial Revolution and the onset of our modern technological societies. Two papers below bear on a prime episode in the story of steam at sea, the achievement of propulsion by screw propeller driven by steam engines. As Dr Greenhill (who suggested this topic for the Dartington conference) says in an introduction to his and Dr Lambert's papers, steam propulsion at sea was principally a British story, made up of a complex sequence of events which most published accounts oversimplify. In his view such a far-reaching development in man's affairs deserves far more rigorous and inter-disciplinary study by historians, engineers and others than it has so far received.

Both papers investigate the attempts to move from the paddle steamer to the more efficient screw propulsion in the 1840s. Thus Basil Greenhill is concerned with a particular and little-known instance of the new means of propulsion, as incorporated in the merchant steamship the *Great Northern*, built and launched at Londonderry in 1842 by an entrepreneurial Canadian shipbuilder, William Coppin (deserving it would seem of study in his own right). Francis Pettit Smith, the patentee of the Archimedes screw propeller and the British pioneer of screw propulsion, was closely associated with her construction. At 1360 tons, the *Great Northern* was then by far the largest screw propelled steamship – or more exactly a steam auxiliary sailing vessel – and in conception at least can be thought of as the first screw frigate, with forty ports for 18 pounder guns. She was distinguished too by being the first steamship to have her engines and boilers in the after part of the construction. Her story offers a fascinating case study of the difficulties faced in bringing about this major innovation in steam propulsion. William Coppin had had her built not to commission but on a speculative basis, in the hope of an Admiralty purchase or at least a charter. But the Admiralty was not forthcoming, partly it seems because of the difficulties that were experienced with her engines and partly because the navy was already involved with a screw vessel being built to their own specification, the *Rattler*. The paper thus contains most interesting contemporary evidence on this experimental stage of screw propulsion (how fascinating if the *trieres* had been so reported in its development stage!).

Dr Greenhill's paper informs us a little also on the Admiralty's relations with the private shipbuilding sector of the day. This relationship is also treated in Dr Lambert's paper, whose main purpose though is to focus on the attitude of the

2

Royal Navy to the adoption of screw propulsion. His is a revisionist paper, concerned to rebut the conventionally-held view that the Admiralty in its prejudice and ignorance deliberately hampered the pioneering efforts to adopt the new steam engine, a view first seriously challenged by Admiral Brock and Basil Greenhill in 1973.[3]

In a detailed discussion which draws heavily on Admiralty and other primary records, Dr Lambert argues that, in the main, naval officers and their political masters had a very clear idea of what they wanted to achieve with steam, and that their caution in the face of an unproven technology should not be condemned. The Admiralty were conscious of their responsibility for the defence of an empire, based on the maintenance of naval supremacy. The real problem as Dr Lambert sees it, was more one of the Admiralty's recently reformed administrative structure and changes in political personnel, not decision making as such. Dr Lambert marshals much evidence to justify this more positive judgement of the Admiralty, reviewing its attitudes towards contemporary tactics, screw propulsion and the various experiments under way, including its own trial vessels, and touches on the role of Brunel in all this. Before 1850 not one of the ships was entirely successful owing to a combination of poor machinery and limited hydrodynamic knowledge. But much empirical data was gained, necessary for the building of an auxiliary steam navy.

Dr Lambert's revisionist arguments are really quite impressive. His examination of the primary evidence puts the Admiralty in a far better light, and, like Dr Greenhill's paper, is revealing on the year to year, trial and error, progress made in establishing this revolutionary form of propulsion, not really achieved in the navy's sphere until the perfection of the screw line of battleship in 1851.

Dr Corlett, who chaired the conference sessions on steam propulsion, offered some summing-up remarks, which are also printed below. From his viewpoint as a naval architect and engineer it is interesting to see his emphatic reiteration of the basic importance of the development of screw propulsion, and to weigh his comment that the powerful economy of today's world shipping depends not only on the size of vessels but on screw propulsion. In his view, proper understanding of this innovation in the mid-nineteenth century requires not only study of the screw propeller and more efficient engines but a whole range of related technical developments, better metals for boilers, better engineering such as efficient surface condensers and improved stern bearings, far better lubricants. All were essential for successful and increasingly efficient steam propulsion.

Dr Corlett also argues, with Basil Greenhill, that proper understanding of such an innovation as steam screw propulsion, deserves much fuller investigation, of a collaborative inter-disciplinary nature. Dr Greenhill did in fact indicate that Exeter University, with its developing interests in maritime historical research, might be a suitable location for such research. Hopefully this may prove to be so, for the University has just established a Research Centre for Maritime Historical Studies, with the present editor and Dr Michael Duffy of the Department of History and Archaeology, a naval historian, as co-directors. One of our major projects may well focus on steam at sea, its achievement and its implications for our modern age.

Stephanie Jones' paper also deals with innovation in shipping, but in a more negative sense than the contribution just discussed. Her discussion centres on tardy

3

recognition of the need for change, or short-sighted priorities, in the British shipping group, P & O, in the 1920s. This was a decade of difficult business conditions and much technological change: Dr Jones considers the policies pursued by the Earl of Inchcape, the group's chairman and its driving force.[4] In his earlier years as a businessman, Lord Inchcape had been a successful British mercantile and shipping entrepreneur on the Indian sub-continent and elsewhere. But as chairman of P & O, one of the largest shipping combines in the world, and at the pinnacle of his fame, his management of the group displayed a curious lack of vision. The paper further offers some interesting reflections on the waning of the British mercantile fleet as a whole in this decade.

Over the 1920s there was notable tonnage growth and innovation in many countries' shipping fleets, with P & O and Britain as a whole lagging behind. As Dr Jones points out, for the longer period, 1914-38, only Britain and Germany experienced net tonnage decreases while, admittedly often from relatively low bases and with favourable opportunities for growth, United States tonnage grew fourfold, Japanese tonnage trebled, and the fleets of Norway, Italy and Greece at least doubled. Inchcape's management of P & O is revealing for understanding this British decline. Between 1914 and 1918 he had been dexterity itself in overcoming wartime problems. He was still ingenious in the 'twenties, but in the face of the real problems facing P & O he looked backwards. His fundamental concern, in a decade of declining profitability brought about by rising costs and competition from other countries, was short-term and financial: by a series of financial expedients he strove to maintain P & O's dividend and keep its share price bouyant. Too little priority was given to the exploitation of the new technologies. P & O's inadequate recognition of the possibilities for innovation – to seize, for instance, the opportunities offered by oil as a power source and a freight for vessels – was paralleled in other British shipping lines and, of course, had serious implications for British shipbuilding, at the time and later. For it was out of the difficulties and depression facing British shipbuilders in the 1930s that Dr Hilditch, in a previous Dartington paper, found in part the origins of the pessimistic 'no growth strategy' or outlook characterising British shipbuilders in the post-1945 era.[5]

As in all good papers perhaps, Dr Jones raises in the reader's mind a desire for more discussion. One would have liked, for instance, to see more consideration of Lord Inchcape's advanced age – he was 70 in 1922 – and whether this and the great length of his business experience played any part in the stultification of his business vision. Dr Jones talks briefly of British shipping in the inter-war years as run predominantly by an older generation constantly harking back to the pre-war days, reluctantly recognising major shifts in trade and technology compared to the 'new shipping men' emerging in Scandinavia and elsewhere. Fuller comparative discussion of this and other possible factors would be profitable. Was the management of other countries' shipping lines in fact in the hands of younger men, how did they see the future in the early 1920s, how did they acquire more 'modern' or far-sighted views?   Were they, for example, helped by a greater resort to commercial intelligence and business forecasting?   In part these questions are treated in a paper on 'Norwegian Shipowning in the Inter-War Years' by Helge

Nordvik and Lewis Fischer given at the 1988 Dartington conference and which is being prepared for the next volume of conference papers. Dr Jones, meanwhile, has made another cogent and stimulating contribution for which she deserves our congratulations.

We now turn to the two papers which relate to innovation in trade. The first, by Alison Grant, offers a well-researched, biographical study of John Delbridge, a Barnstaple merchant of the early seventeenth century. This was a time of epoch-making innovation in English overseas commerce, in particular the opening-up of trade with North America and Asia. With the associated innovations in commodity composition , shipping and commercial organisation, the period can be viewed as the beginning of the English 'Commercial Revolution', with its notable, some would say profound, implications for later English economic growth, including the classic Industrial Revolution.[6] John Delbridge was one of the earliest promoters of English North American settlement and trade, and Dr Grant provides us with as thorough and rounded an appreciation of this pioneering merchant as the surviving sources are likely to permit.

Delbridge was born into a commercially innovative environment. Barnstaple merchants over the sixteenth century had a good record in developing new trades – the marketing of dried codfish from the Newfoundland fisheries to Portugal and Spain; the exchange of English products for the wines and fruits of the Atlantic Islands – Madeira, the Canaries and the Azores; and with other Devon or Devon-connected merchants the establishment of the first English Guinea Company, bartering manufactures for men to be enslaved into the New World. Delbridge, son of a middling Barnstaple merchant and son-in-law of a leading local merchant, himself entered active commerce in 1590 and for almost fifty years pursued a successful business career. Initially in the French, Irish and coastal trades, he soon branched out into the Spanish and Atlantic Isles commerce. His claim to fame though began with his becoming a member of the London Virginia Company in 1612, six years after its establishment. In 1620 he sent out to the new colony in the 100-ton *Swan* of Barnstaple, 71 'choice men ... out of Devonshire ... brought up to Husbandry', and thereafter was active in a succession of emigration ventures to Virginia, Bermuda and New England, his ships engaged also in inter-colonial commerce and bringing back cargoes of tobacco and other commodities to Barnstaple. Dr Grant is revealing on the independent character and lively public persona of the man. One of the 'hotter sorts of protestants', with a respect for learning, he was a doughty local politician and Member of Parliament, and an ardent campaigner for contemporary 'free trade', the rights of provincial men to trade where they wished against the overweening interests of London merchants. Dr Grant has substantially added to our stock of understanding of the enterprising merchant class of the reigns of James I and Charles I.

Arthur Clark's paper also explores British enterprise in the actual opening-up of trades and ports, this time on the South African coast east of the Cape of Good Hope in the early nineteenth century. Dr Clark is a historical geographer who lectures at Rhodes University, Grahamstown: his contribution comes out of his research into South Africa's history. His essay very well illustrates the inexorable

5

march of Western man over the centuries into sparsely settled areas of the world with commercial potential, bringing them into both a local and international economy. Like Dr Grant's essay on Delbridge, it reveals the cutting edge of European expansion, on the frontier, the process by which 'Europe transformed the economic and social pattern of much of the world', in William Woodruff's words.[7]

In 1795 when the Dutch settlement at the Cape of Good Hope was occupied by the British, the new administration began to take up vigorously what the Dutch had done little about, an assessment of possible ports on the east coast. The Cape then had little developed local trades or supplies: 'we found the colony destitute of almost everything', wrote one British administrator. It was hoped that with government support in the form of further surveying of harbours and tidal rivers along the coast, 'the spirit of private adventure will induce merchants to supply the market of the Cape with every article of European produce'. This combination of public but principally private enterprise in time achieved much; by 1840 six new ports had been established, substantial amounts of capital had been invested in installations and shipping, and a variety of trades, inward and outward, involving foodstuffs, wool and timber, and European manufactures as well as settlers, had been established. It was hoped to introduce Cape wines into England, even though, rather dauntingly, a speaker in the House of Commons had thought them 'a drink only suitable for tipplers and bargemen'. A particular merit of Dr Clark's work is the summary biographical treatment he gives to the thirty or so merchants, British very largely, prominent in this achievement, their backgrounds, activities and degrees of success. He draws well on the abundant printed primary material now available, as a result of the considerable South African interest in the early settlers. Some of these entrepreneurs were already in trade, others were landowners who turned to trade to market their produce, others came from seafaring, including naval, occupations. Some were to lose their lives on these generally inhospitable shores. Dr Clark reveals well the innovative vigour and determination of British enterprise of this period in an alien setting, a setting quite different from 'the frames of reference brought from northern seas'.

The final contribution to this volume, by David Williams, while not relating directly to our theme of innovation in shipping or trade, does, however, argue the case for more innovation in maritime historical investigation: its purpose is to call for greater recognition of the commercial picture postcard as a source. As Mr Williams points out there is a general reluctance among historians to use visual sources: while ignorance of (or indifference to) the humble picture postcard is worsened by problems of its accessibility. Despite its long-established attraction for personal collectors, in the main archival collections have only comparatively recently begun to be formed.

In its 'golden age', from 1894 to the 1920s, the picture postcard was produced commercially in very great numbers indeed, on an infinite variety of subjects. As Mr Williams states, it is 'in fact, the greatest source of visual record' in early twentieth-century Europe, or for that matter the world. He considers that for the maritime historian, the picture postcard has value not only as a visual record of maritime affairs but as an historical artefact in its own right, for example, as

6

shipping company advertising, and as a conveyor of popular attitudes, for instance, of the seaman or of enemies in time of war. The postcards selected for illustration eminently fulfil their purpose, although their impact in some cases has necessarily if sadly been somewhat reduced by the need for reproduction in black and white rather than their original, often vivid, colour.

Mr Williams indubitably makes his case: clearly the picture postcard, helped by such advocacy, will come more into its own as twentieth-century maritime studies burgeon. The paper brings to mind an earlier Dartington conference contribution of 1973, by John Gilman,[8] who made a plea both for more use of photographs and more archival preservation and cataloguing, demonstrating his point for port research with some fine photographs of Porlock Weir in Somerset in late Victorian and Edwardian times. We may add, that the potential for witnessing the past through the agency of privately-taken photographs continues to expand with the increasing proliferation of the cheap camera, while the potential use of film has been transformed by the growth of film and television company archive material. Currently there is a new development also of great potential impact. For the coming of the personal video camera will mean in time a super-abundance of supply of movie images on all possible manner of themes, for use by the maritime, as other species of, historian.

July 1989   Stephen Fisher

NOTES

1   See editor's introduction in Stephen Fisher, ed., *Lisbon as a Port Town, the British Seaman and other Maritime Themes* (Exeter, 1988).

2   J. S. Morrison and J. F. Coates, *The Athenian Trireme. The History and Reconstruction of an Ancient Greek Warship*(Cambridge, 1986), 1-4. The general significance of the Athenian trireme, its evolution and eventual supersession, are discussed in Chapters 1 and 2. The work also tells, technically and in its historical setting, of the thinking behind the recent reconstruction of a *trieres*.

3   P. W. Brock and Basil Greenhill, *Sail and Steam* (Newton Abbot, 1973).

7

4   Dr Jones has recently published a series of works on Lord Inchcape, including a paper from an earlier Dartington conference, 'British Mercantile Enterprise Overseas in the Nineteenth Century: the Example of James Lyle Mackay, First Earl of Inchcape' – for the full references, see Notes 1-3 of her paper below.

5   Peter Hilditch, 'The Decline of British Shipbuilding since the Second World War', in Fisher, ed., *Lisbon as a Port Town*, 129-42.

6   Among the many discussions of early modern commercial change see, Ralph Davis, *The Commercial Revolution* (London, 1967); the papers collected and edited by W. E. Minchinton, *The Growth of English Overseas Trade in the Seventeenth and Eighteenth Centuries* (London, 1969), including the editor's introduction; and for more critical recent views, R. P. Thomas and D. N. McCloskey, 'Overseas Trade and Empire 1700-1860', in Roderick Floud and Donald McCloskey, eds, *The Economic History of Britain since 1700*, Vol. 1, 1700-1860 (Cambridge,1981), 87-102, and Patrick O'Brien, 'European Economic Development: the Contribution of the Periphery', *Economic History Review*, Sec. Ser., XXXV (1982), 1-18.

7   William Woodruff, *Impact of Western Man. A Study of Europe's Role in the World Economy 1750-1960* (London, 1966).

8   John Gilman, 'Photographic Source Material for the History of Ports', in H.E.S. Fisher and W.E. Minchinton, eds, *Transport and Shipowning in the Westcountry* (Exeter, 1973), 69-83.

SOME POSSIBLE TECHNICAL FEATURES OF A SALAMIS *TRIERES*

Keith Hamilton-Smith and Ewan Corlett

The considerable correspondence in *The Times* in 1975 debating the performance capabilities of the triremes that fought the Salamis action and the more recent interest culminating in the construction of a full-scale replica shows the continued fascination exercised by these vessels. It can be argued that in technical terms the building of oared warships reached a peak in that period and that, while they became larger and more complex later, in some respects they never again reached the perfection achieved around 400 BC.

Basic material on the subject has been collected by a considerable number of researchers in the last fifty years or so, for example, Rados in France, Foley and Soedel recently in America, and in particular Morrison.[1] They have analysed the available archaelogical evidence in considerable detail. Morrison[2] and Rados[3] drew attention to the Zea ship-sheds and the light that they throw on the dimensions of a *trieres*. Furthermore, having produced approximate dimensions for the vessel, Morrison went on to analyse the layout of oarsmen and produced the only one that stands up to detailed technical examination.[4] Increasingly this layout is being adopted as the most probable, and indeed is so in this text. Morrison's work led to the important 'Athenian Trireme' project involving the proposed construction of a full-scale prototype in Greece.[5]

The Trireme project has been carried to completion, in the successful building in Greece of a full-scale replica. Both in terms of general and detailed design this ship is clearly a close approximation to the original, and all those connected with the project have much with which to congratulate themselves. Exact dimensions and some details remain, of course, a matter of opinion, and the Appendix to this work shows the approximate comparative dimensions of the Morrison/Coates (hereafter M/C) *trieres*[6] and of the design covered by the present authors.

The rowing performance of the replica so far, it would seem, has been somewhat disappointing, partly due, one must imagine, to the sheer difficulty of assembling, training and practising so many oarsmen. The purely fixed-seat nature of the propulsion of this replica is probably another factor, and may indeed be one major factor affecting performance – the reasons for this are considered below.

Adopting then the general concept set out in the references in note 4, the authors attempted an *ab initio* approach in 1980-1981 to analyse the basic technical parameters of a *trieres*. This work was completed in 1982 and provides an interesting comparison with the M/C work. The similarities of the conclusive designs are encouraging and afford confidence in the basic reconstruction philosophies.

The main thrust of the present paper is limited, that is to show that a *trieres* may well have been fitted with a primitive form of sliding seat, that the main offensive weapon – the ram – would not and could not have been aligned parallel to the keel or baseline, and furthermore that the historically-quoted performances were indeed possible.

Proportions

As overall premises, it seems likely that the vessel would be undecked generally;[7] that in battle it would be stripped down, leaving masts, sails and other irrelevant equipment ashore;[8] and that generally it would be kept out of the water to minimise water absorption. Triremes were built for speed,[9] and this fits well with the requirement to haul the vessels out of the water as lightness and length are prerequisites of both.

As regards general proportions, the clear distance between the stone columns in the Zea ship-sheds was 6 metres (19 ft. 6 ins.),[10] while the dry length of the slipways was approximately 37 metres (121 ft. 6 ins.) according to Morrison,[11] and around 45 metres (150 ft.) according to Rados.[12] The latter specifically comments upon the uncertainty of this measurement in view of the destruction of the site. The slipways were laid at a slope of 1:10,[13] which appears to be a sensible value to choose. The depth of water over the end of the slipway is indeterminate, but, as will be shown later, need not exceed 0.6 – 0.7 metres (2 ft.).

An unmistakable trend in all warships, as development of a type proceeds, is to build up to the limit of the physical restraints. A good example of this was the limitation on the dimensions of British battleships, particularly breadth, imposed by graving docks in British ports. The breadth of such ships rapidly approached the limit and was constrained thereafter, at perhaps undesirably low levels, in successive classes. It can be taken, therefore, as likely that by the time a Salamis *trieres* was housed in the Zea ship-sheds its dimensions would have increased to the point where the sheds themselves offered a limit. That being so, it seems reasonable to take the clearance between the outriggers (*parexeiresia*) and the columns as being the minimum through which a man could squeeze comfortably, say 36 cm., (14 ins.). This fixes the breadth overall at 5.22 metres (17.12 ft.). M/C arrive at a slightly greater overall breadth – approaching 5.5 metres.

The vessel would be berthed stern first, as on a beach, and accordingly the bow might be expected to tange with the slipway on top of the runners approximately at the slipway waterline. On launching the bow would be afloat in about 0.61 m. (2 ft.) of water. This gives a 'Morrison' extreme length overall of 40 metres (131 ft.) with a 'Rados' length extreme of 45 m. (147 ft.). The M/C reconstruction has a length of under 40 m. at 36.8 m.

The need for as much length as possible becomes apparent when the vessel is laid out in terms of an acceptable rowing module i.e. repeating space between

10

successive rowers, allowing for reasonable plan view curvature of the oar levels fore and aft. The overhang of the outriggers has been taken by Morrison as 0.61 metres (2 ft.) each,[14] this figure has been used in deriving dimensions. The breadth over the hull, therefore, would be 4.0 metres (13.1 ft.) (The M/C reconstruction breadth over the hull is 4.6 m., i.e. with a reduced overhang).

Weight

It is clear that these vessels were shallow drafted. They were hauled up on beaches at night and indeed certainly stern first. As the ship sheds were built at a slope of 1:10 it is very likely that some form of mechanical advantage was used, perhaps block and tackle or a winch or something similar to the log windlass common until recently in small wooden sailing vessels. On beaches, however, the hauling power would be limited to the crew. A commonly accepted figure for a man pulling on a rope is 25-41 kg.f. (56-90 lbs.f.) per man.[15]

Taking the latter figure, for after all the men involved were fit warriors, and the beach at a declivity of 1:40, with a coefficient of friction of say 0.1 for an oak keel running on greased transverse timbers, and postulating that say 180 men must be capable of pulling the vessel out of the water, one can produce an estimate of the weight. The pull produced on the ropes would be 7380 kg.f. (16,240 lbs.f.) and this would lead to a weight of say 58 tonnes.

At a later stage in this work, based upon the subsequently produced lines plan and arrangement drawing and upon the wood construction commonly accepted, i.e. keel – oak, frames – pine or oak, interior – larch or plane, and the remainder – fir, pine or cypress, the basic hull weight has been calculated, assuming picked timbers, well dried and not allowed to soak. The total dry weight of the complete hull, the ram, seating, decks, the *epotides* (bow or ear timbers) and the oars works out at about 35 tonnes. This excludes the masting and rigging. As regards the deadweight, about 70 kg. (155 lbs.) per man equipped seems reasonable giving 14 tonnes for crew plus another 3 tonnes for provisions etc. Thus in battle condition the overall displacement on these calculations would be about 52 tonnes: this is close to the M/C figure of 50 tonnes. In the deep load condition the overall displacement would be about 65 tonnes, and a reasonable average condition in cruising would accord with the earlier figure derived from pulling up a beach.

A picture of the vessel now begins to emerge. The dimensions must be close to correct and the displacement cannot be far wrong.

From the Zea ship-sheds it is clear that the draft of the vessel must have been moderate, probably not much more than 1.0 m. (3.3 ft.) loaded. This would give a reasonable beaching condition so that men could work in water, up to say their navels, when pulling the ship ashore initially.

Layout

There is ample evidence available as to the general layout of the vessels once the proportions and weight have been decided. However, a decision was necessary as to whether the midships section might have embodied deadrise or not.

For convenience, when pulling up in the ship sheds, the weight was probably taken on a central keel with only light locating loads taken on the bilges or on side runners. On beaches it would be most undesirable to haul up on two rows of keels as this could much increase the pull required from the crew.

There are numerous references in the literature to *hermata*.[16] These apparently were long piles of stones used to pack up the ship and were clearly temporary bilge shores to prevent the vessel falling over. It seems certain that in order to be able to get such stones into position, a moderate deadrise would be necessary and anyway the vessel with a fine form would have fairly slack bilges. Figure 1 shows the general proportions of the vessel as envisaged by the authors and, in cross section, the *hermata* supporting the bilges on beaches. Greased hides may have been laid on top of the *hermata*.

An interesting feature of some of the classical representations is the arrangement of the bronze ram. This is well shown in some Greek coins of the period. Plates 20 and 27 of Note 1 show these clearly. The angles of the rams, and their supporting lugs are not parallel to the keel but inclined upwards as they go aft. Of course, this could be simply poor draughtsmanship, but it seems more likely to be a carefully designed technical feature.

Figure 2 shows our derived lines plan for an Athenian *trieres*. On this is shown the centre line for the ram and its supports, projected back to amidships. This line goes through the calculated centre of gravity of the vessel and so it should. If this vessel should ram another and the line of thrust were parallel to the keel then the ram reaction would produce a couple about the centre of gravity tending to make the vessel pitch downwards sharply at the bow. At 10 knots this downward pitch would produce a vertical shearing force of around 3 tonnes on the ram. The load, therefore, would be taken not only as a thrust along the axis of the ram but also partly as a vertical force through the ram tending to tear it off the bow. If, however, the line of thrust through the ram and its supports, spreading the load to the hull, should project to the centre of gravity it is clear that no such moment could arise and the collision force would be taken purely as a thrust along the supports of the ram with no transverse component. This is a simple, ingenious feature and a necessary one.

The ram would be a 'wishbone-shaped' shoe – two arms fitting around the stem with the ram itself projecting forward of the stem proper. The latter would be a heavy vertical timber into which the keel and the upper stem would be scarphed. Clearly there would be heavy side stringers in way of the ram which would then bed against the forward edge of a heavy stem timber while the two side extensions would be through-bolted onto the stringers etc. This is shown in Figure 1. This shape is well arranged for smoothly decelerated ramming, the need for which is probably the reason for the horn-like projections on the ram itself, spreading the load progressively as the *trieres* penetrated its target. Deceleration from 10 knots to rest during say half a second would be about 1 g. which is quite reasonable. M/C quote, by comparison, 10 knots over 1 metre distance which is not dissimilar.

The *epotides* are known to have been at the level of the *pexeiresia* and must have had brackets taking the bottom of each *epotis* down onto the hull proper. Thus each *epotis* would protect the forward end of its outrigger and as the whole structure continued right across the ship the centre would form the rearmost support of the fore and aft timber supporting the upper stem. The primary load upon an *epotis* would be directed aft with a secondary force upwards. The bracing is well adapted to these loads.

Figure 1a shows an hypothetical reconstruction of the stern structure. It is conceivable that this type of stern was evolved from the original reed forms. Pre-8th century sewn construction would have led to the necessity for lapping gunwales over planks and finally gunwale over gunwale as restricted space would prevent the normal internal lashings being made. The final lashings would probably have been external to the stern post which would account for the *aphoston*.

With mortice and tenon construction the number of gunwales carried into the *aphoston* could be reduced and with the pinning and dove-tailing of them to a stern post the original lashing point might have been retained as a purely decorative feature. This is shown on Figure 1a, which also shows the fulcrum and box lashing for the steering oar. From experience it would seem that this arrangement would be suitable for tension adjustment through the frapping turns on the lashing between the fulcrum and the steering oar. The arrangement also would allow the oar to be raised as is indeed shown in many illustrations.

Figure 3 shows the hydrostatics or curves of form for this hypothetical reconstruction of a *trieres*. At 52 tons displacement the block or fullness coefficient would be about 0.48 and the prismatic coefficient about 0.69. In the load condition the same coefficients would be 0.5 and just over 0.7. As will be seen later, these are suitable figures to meet the performances needed for the voyages quoted by Xenophon in particular.[17]

Rowing Arrangement

The detailed design of the vessel is likely of course to be centred around the rowing arrangements and these indeed are of real interest, both in concept and in their effect on performance. The basic factor is the rowing module which determines the direct relationship between the length of the vessel and the number of oarsmen. Some experiments have been made by the authors to determine an acceptable rowing module and this was found to be 0.94 metres (37 ins.).

In side elevation, perhaps the best guide as to arrangement is given by the Lenormant relief preserved in the National Museum, Athens. This is illustrated in Plates 23 and 24 of Note 1. In Figure 4, the dotted lines show the position required for the outrigger supports in a vertical line to clear the oars. Incidentally, only when looking down on the oars in plan view or at an angle from fore and aft would they appear to be parallel. This relief also shows the angle between the thighs and calf of the oarsmen at the forward position.

There seems to be reason to believe, on hydrodynamic and historical grounds, that a primitive form of sliding seat may have been used in a *trieres*. Part of the equipment of each oarsman was the so-called *'huperesion'*.[18] This is interpreted by Morrison as a cushion on which the oarsmen would sit and a pad to save him from the consequences of rowing. Now on purely mechanical grounds, the effort required from the oarsmen would appear to require a certain amount of fore and aft slide and, interestingly, the Lenormant relief and the Roman relief from Aquila (Plate 23b of Note 1) both show leg positions, i.e. the angles between the thighs, calves and torso, at the start of the stroke consistent with a moderate degree of forward movement on a sliding seat and not with a fixed seat.

It is postulated that the *huperesion* was gripped between the buttocks and slid on a greased fore and aft protrusion rather like an elongated bicycle saddle. Figures 5a and 5b show how this could be arranged and this fits well with the module previously determined. This projection forward of the thwart need not be a stringer as suggested by M/C, but simply a quite portable addition to the thwart. The projection could drop into a fastening on the thwart and be supported by a short strut at its forward end, extending down into a recess in the deck below; in other words, rather like a commonly adopted form of helmsman's seat today.

Figure 6a shows the profile at the start of the stroke. This figure has been revised for perspective. It was found in preparing it that to ensure that the thalamian oar tip did not foul the tip of the thranite oar in the next group, at the end of the stroke, the thalamian oar port must be 1.14 metres forward of the thalamian thole pin. Figure 6b shows the relative positions of the oarsmen at the start of the stroke. When placed upon the revised profile a thranite can be seen clearly in the upper portion of the vessel with his legs hidden by the framing. The support for his seat lines up with the short stanchion in the second third of the out rigger space. A zugian is practically hidden from view, being inboard of a thranite and only part of his back and a glimpse of his hands would show at this moment. The thalamian is completely hidden by the sides of the vessel. It should be noted that the oarsmen would be in a similar attitude when at rest on their oars. The layout of the oars in plan view, in this situation at the start of the stroke, is shown in Figure 6c. The relative position of the rowers is shown in Figure 7a in profile and 7b in plan view. The appearance of the oarsmen from the side at this point is shown in Figure 7c. Finally, the position at the end of the stroke is shown in Figures 8a, b and c. The total angular movement of an oar, is between 40° and 50°.

In Figure 8b it will be seen that in some instances thranite and zugian oars may cross as shown by chain dotted lines. This is acceptable as reference to the midships section, Figure 9, shows that the zugian oars should always lie inboard and clear of the thranite oars.

It will be seen that the awning posts curve outwards so that in action the leather or quilting would hang loose from the side giving better protection than if taut. These posts are shown curved which would indeed seem to be the simplest method of construction, the feet lying parallel to the frames and lapped to them.

14

The Lenormant relief shows what are clearly curved awning posts and deck supports and this is repeated in Plate 26b of Note 1.

The outriggers may have been straight or curved: there is evidence in various representations of both. Figure 10 shows a reconstruction of the curved type of structure. The zugian oar would touch the rigger support at the start of the stroke, if the support were vertical. This suggests that the supports may have had a similar slope to the oars in profile, in other words the bottom being rather forward of the top. This layout appears to work and to give the opportunity for the oarsmen to develop the power of a semi-sliding seat without any mechanical complications.

An interesting and technically sound analysis of the theory of rowing is given by Alexander.[19] In a detailed engineering analysis of the performance of a rowing eight and a naval whaler he shows that the sliding seat boat enables its crew to produce an output of approximately 1.1 horsepower continuously over a period of say 20 minutes and the fixed seat boat under 0.9 horsepower per man. Outputs of this order, or more, have been determined experimentally by measuring oxygen consumption. The eight achieved approximately 10 knots at this horsepower and the whaler about $6^3/_4$ knots. However, not only did the sliding seat arrangement permit a greater output of power, but also a higher propulsive efficiency, approximately 32 per cent as against 22 per cent. The main reason for this is that the unproductive work caused by acclerating the bodies and oars as a proportion of the total work is less in the case of the eight than in the whaler. Furthermore, in the eight the oar maintains its peak thrust over an appreciable part of the power stroke whereas the whaler oar reaches a peak of thrust and rapidly falls away from that peak.

In the case of the *trieres*, the overall rowing efficiency might be expected to be rather closer to that of the whaler than the eight, but because of the high ship speed and the modest sliding seat movement (approximately 8 inches of slide) there would be some improvement. The ratio of inboard to outboard parts of the oar is important. This ratio is about 0.41 for an eight, about 0.26 for a whaler and ranges from 0.40 for thranite to 0.48 for zugian oarsmen in a *trieres*. Their oars appear to be rather longer than those of the eight and the whaler, the excess being about 1.4 ft. and 0.8 ft. respectively.

The angle through which the oar is moved during the stroke is rather poor in the case of the *trieres*, between 40° and 50° comparing with 48° for the whaler and 80° for the eight. The reason is mainly the relatively high location of the thole pins and the limited slide. The slip of the oar ranges from about 30 per cent with the eight to 36 per cent with the whaler. Alexander defines this slip as the distance the oars move through the water itself during the stroke as they exert their leverage on the boat, and is expressed as a percentage of the travel of the boat during that period.[20] In the case of the *trieres*, this slip might be expected to be about 32 per cent leading to a velocity of the oar handles at 10 knots of about 10 ft.sec. The length of the stroke at the handle can be shown to be about 3.2 ft. so, the duration of the power stroke at 10 knots therefore would be approximately 0.32 seconds.

For good rowing practice the return part of the stroke, for only partially sliding seats, is about 2.5 – 3 times as long as the power portion leading to a striking rate of between 47 and 54 per minute. This is quite high but similar to that of a whaler and shows that a speed of 10 knots could be produced with this configuration.

The propulsion efficiency might be expected to be rather below the mean of those of the eight and the whaler, say 26-27 per cent, while the output of each oarsmen in a sprint might be expected to be higher than that of the whaler but lower than that of the eight. A mean figure of 1 horsepower per man would seem not unreasonable for hard, trained warriors. On the other hand, at lower rates of working the propulsive efficiency would be appreciably higher, probably of the order of 43 per cent in a continuous paddle and double that of the sprint when in a slow paddle. From experience these two modes of working represent approximately 25 and 15 per cent of maximum power output per man respectively.

The products therefore of these efficiencies and outputs give useful horse-powers (U.H.P.) as follows:

170 oarsmen sprinting for up to 20 minutes	44
Same crew in a continuous paddle	17.5
Same crew in a slow paddle	12.4

Performance

The actual performance capabilities of a *trieres* can be explored quite simply using systematic tank test data. With a relatively fine block coefficient and a high length/breadth ratio the so-called Taylor/Gertler[22] series affords a good basis for resistance estimation. It should be noted that the vessel has a quite modern bow shape with an hydrodynamic ram (as in the original of the series) and a length/breadth ratio similar to the basic ship in the series.

A very interesting feature can be determined from this series when analysing vessels of considerable length and light displacement. The displacement length ratio can be described in a number of ways, that used in Taylor/Gertler takes the volumetric displacement, in cubic feet, divided by the cube of the waterline length in feet. It has been found from previous analyses,[23] that if the volumetric coefficient is appreciably less than 2×10^{-3}, two curious features appear in the residuary or wave making resistance of the vessel.

In parenthesis, the bulk of the resistance through the water of a ship is a combination of skin friction, i.e. the rubbing of the hull against the water as it goes through it, and wave making, the latter creating the well known V-shaped divergent wave trains at bow and stern and the transverse wave train at the stern in the wake. At high speeds wave making dominates and indeed provides a limit to the possible speed from any given length of high speed displacement vessel. Fully submerged vessels, such as nuclear submarines, can attain very high speeds for their length because they do not make waves, but the surface vessel is nearly always limited by its wave making propensities.

Fast planing boats get over this to some extent by lifting themselves out of the water dynamically, and the same can be said of hydrofoils and hovercraft.

However, if a displacement vessel, which does not lift itself out of the water or submerge itself fully, has a really low volumetric coefficient, then above a certain speed/length ratio, that is speed divided by the root of the length, the residuary resistance coefficient can become constant and furthermore independent of the prismatic coefficient. (The latter defines the fullness of the ends of the vessel). This phenomenon means that the hull can be designed for minimum wetted surface and hence of low skin friction. These are two interesting features and almost certainly were part of the inherent hydrodynamic characteristics of a *trieres*.

Taking the displacement of the vessel derived earlier, in the cruise and battle conditions respectively at 65 and about 50 tons, the corresponding volumetric coefficients are 1.34×10^{-3} and 1.05×10^{-3}. These are low and suitable for high speed propulsion, with little wavemaking.

It is interesting that the dug-out canoes of England and Wales show that four out of the 24 reconstructed[24] show volumetric coefficients below 2×10^{-3}. The others are very much higher. The inference is that four of the 24 were fast fighting boats, the remainder were cargo carriers. Similarly, Viking longships and Faerings have been shown to have volumetric coefficients in the range of 1.5 to 1.8×10^{-3}. In both the case of a Faering replica and the replica of the Gokstad ship built for Manx Millenium year and which was sailed from Norway to the Isle of Man, this semi-planing characteristic at high speeds has been noted by the crews. The important conclusion can be drawn that a *trieres* was capable of quite high speeds on modest power requirements.

Figure 11 shows the effective horsepower (E.H.P.) calculated as required to drive the ship through the water at speeds of up to about 12 knots. This power is modest, especially in the battle condition. In producing this estimate a quite rough hull has been assumed, the roughness coefficient being equivalent to that of a riveted steel ship. In practice the surface may well have been kept smoother than this. Figure 11 shows the power curves at 65 and 52 tonnes displacement for a 36 metre waterline-length ship, but also shows a curve for a 40 metre ship at 58 tonnes. The beneficial effect of length on propelling the power, at the higher speeds, is apparent.

Superimposed on the horsepower/knots curves are shown the useful horsepower (U.H.P.) levels for three configurations of oarsmen. First at A, 170 oarsmen are shown driving the ship into battle. A continuous speed of 10.6 knots can be maintained (11.5 statute miles per hour), for perhaps 10-15 minutes. At B, the men are in continuous cruise at a power output of 15 per cent of their sprint rating. In this situation 7.2 knots (8.3 mph) can be maintained, almost indefinitely. Finally, at C, 170 oarsmen are shown in a fast cruise which maybe could be maintained for up to 6 hours giving a speed of 8.1 knots (9.3 mph). Thus, it can be seen that a voyage such as that described by Xenophon, of 120 nautical miles, would take just over 16 hours, which seems reasonable.

It does seem possible to conclude, with reasonable certainty, that these ships were in fact capable of battle speeds between 10 and 11 knots and long-distance cruising speeds about two-thirds of that. The level of technological design required to do this was remarkably high, as was what we can deduce to be the structural

17

arrangements of the vessels. As with many such developments, however, considerations other than sheer engineering efficiency eventually took precedence. Later multi-oared ships were of relatively low hydrodynamic efficiency, if much larger and more powerful as warships.

APPENDIX

		Hamilton-Smith/ Corlett	Morrison/Coates
Loa	Length o.a.	40 M.	37 M.
Lwl	Length w.l.	36 M.	34 M.
Bwl	Breadth w.l.	40 M.	37 M.
Boa	Breadth o.a.	5.22 M.	5.4 M.
Depth		1.95 M.	2.1 M.
Draught (Salamis)		0.9– 1.0 M.	1.18 M. extreme moulded
Displacement (Salamis)		50 t.	52 t.

NOTES

1   J.S. Morrison and R.T. Williams, *Greek Oared Ships, 900 – 322 B.C.* (Cambridge, 1968).

2   *Ibid.*, 191.

3   C. Rados, *Les Guerres et Mediques. La Bataille de Salamine* (Paris, 1925).

4   Morrison and Williams, *Greek Oared Ships*, 284 and Plate 25.

5   J.S. Morrison and J.F. Coates, *The Athenian Trireme. The History and Reconstruction of an Ancient Greek Warship* (Cambridge University Press, 1986).

6 *Ibid.,*

7 Thucydides, 1.14; Morrison, *Greek Oared Ships*, 281.

8 *Ibid.,* 298.

9 Plutarch, *Cimon*, 6.

10 Morrison, *Greek Oared Ships*, 182.

11 *Ibid.,* 184.

12 Rados, *Les Guerres*, 82.

13 Morrison, *Greek Oared Ships*, 181.

14 *Ibid.,* 185 and Plate 25.

15 *Admiralty Manual of Seamanship*, 1951.

16 Morrison, *Greek Oared Ships*, 293.

17 *Ibid.,* 309.

18 *Ibid.,* 269.

19 F.H. Alexander, 'The Propulsive Efficiency of Rowing', *Transactions of Royal Institution of Naval Architects*, LXIX (1927).

20 *Ibid.,* 230.

21 *Ibid.,* 232.

22 A Reanalysis of the Original Test Data for the Taylor Standard Series: The David W. Taylor Model Basin.

23 E.C.B. Corlett, 'Twin Hull Ships', *Transactions of Royal Institution of Naval Architects*, CXI (1969); S. McGrail and E.C.B. Corlett, 'The High Speed Capabilities of Ancient Boats', *International Journal of Nautical Archaeology*, 6 (1977).

24 McGrail and Corlett, 'Ancient Boats'.

ATHENIAN TRIERES

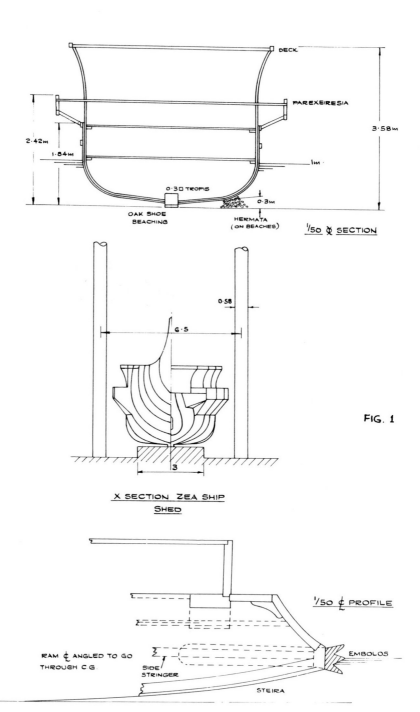

DECK

PAREXEIRESIA

3·58m

2·42m

1·84m

1m

0·3□ TROPIS

OAK SHOE
BEACHING

HERMATA
(ON BEACHES)

0·3m

¹/50 ⚲ SECTION

0·58

6·5

3

X SECTION ZEA SHIP
SHED

FIG. 1

¹/50 ₵ PROFILE

RAM ₵ ANGLED TO GO
THROUGH C.G.

SIDE
STRINGER

EMBOLOS

STEIRA

ATHENIAN TRIERES

L.O.A	40·00 M
B. EXT. OVER PLANK	4·00 M
B. OVERALL	5·22 M
DRAFT LOADED	1·00 M
ROWING MODULE	37″

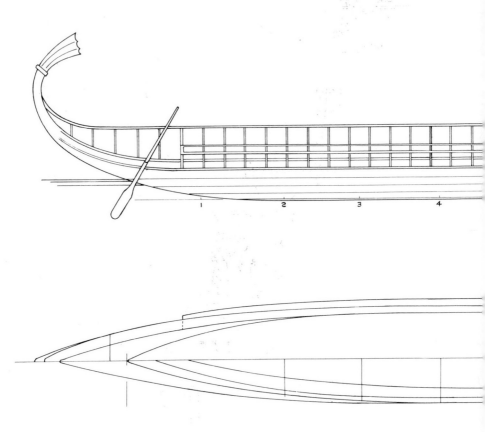

FIG. 1 Cont.

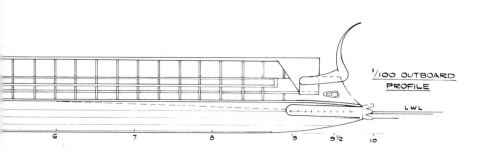

$^1/_{100}$ OUTBOARD
PROFILE

LWL

6   7   8   9   9½   10

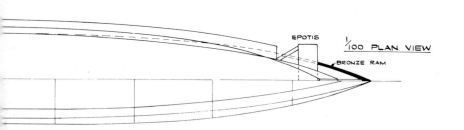

EPOTIS

$^1/_{100}$ PLAN VIEW

BRONZE RAM

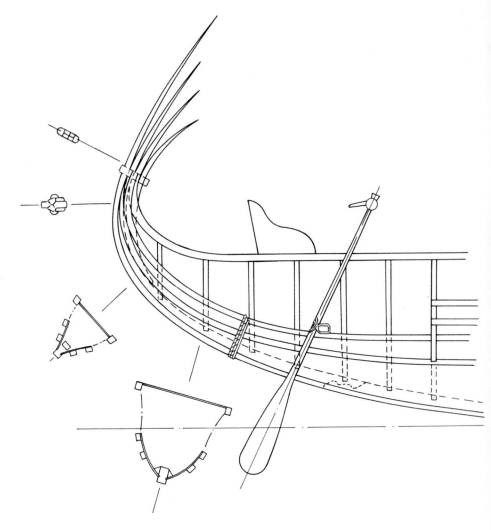

FIG. 1a

ATHENIAN TRIERES LINES PLAN.

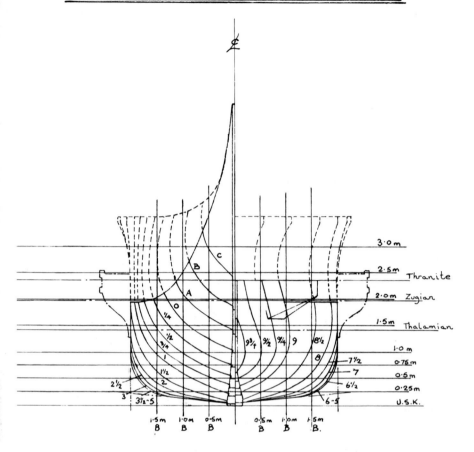

PRINCIPAL DIMENSIONS.

LENGTH O.A. _____ 40·0 m.

LENGTH STA. _____ 35·95 m.

BEAM O.A. _____ 5·22 m.

BEAM EXT. OVER HULL PLANK ___ 4·0 m.

DRAFT LOADED _____ 1·0 m.

DEPTH AMIDSHIPS _____ 1·95 m.

ROWING MODULE _____ 940mm

LINES DRAWN TO OUTSIDE OF PLANK.

FIG. 2

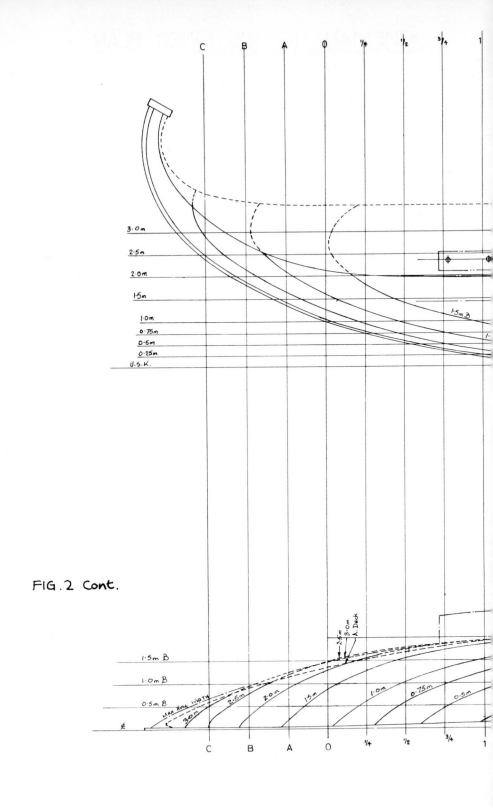

C B A 0 ¼ ½ ¾ 1

3·0m

2·5m

2·0m

1·5m

1·0m

0·75m

0·5m

0·25m

U.S.K.

1·5m B

FIG. 2 Cont.

1·5m B

1·0m B

0·5m B

2·5m 3·0m A. Deck

MAX. HULL WIDTH

3·0m 2·5m 2·0m 1·5m 1·0m 0·75m 0·5m

¢

C B A 0 ¼ ½ ¾ 1

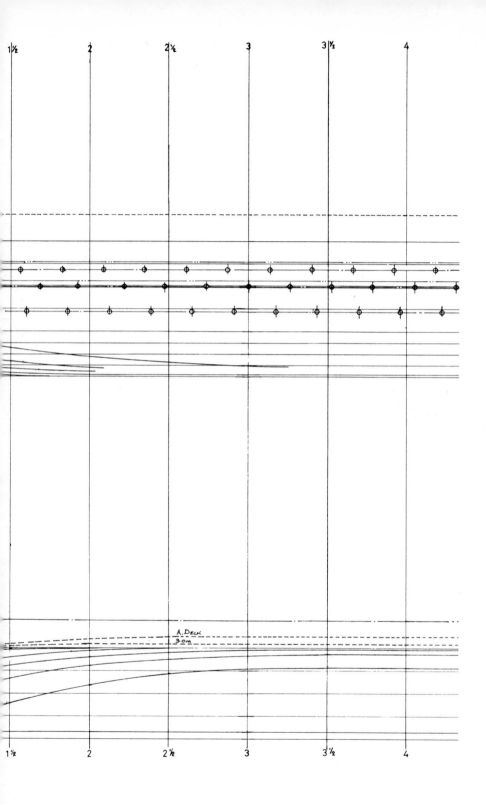

A. DECK
3.0m

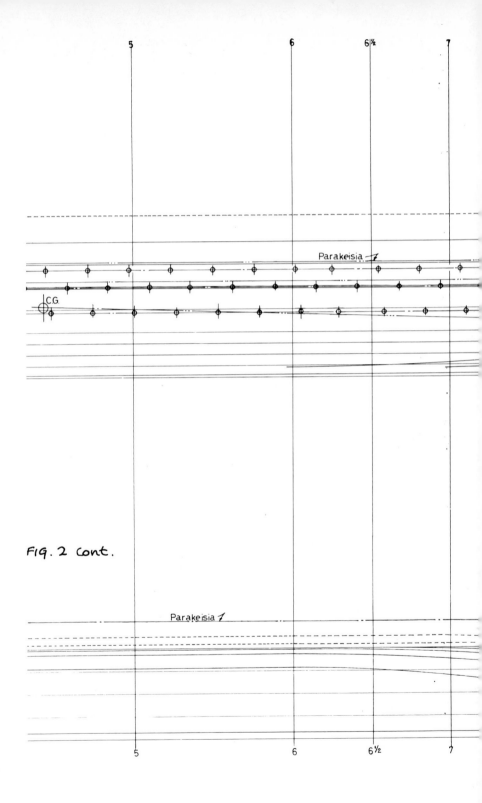

FIG. 2 cont.

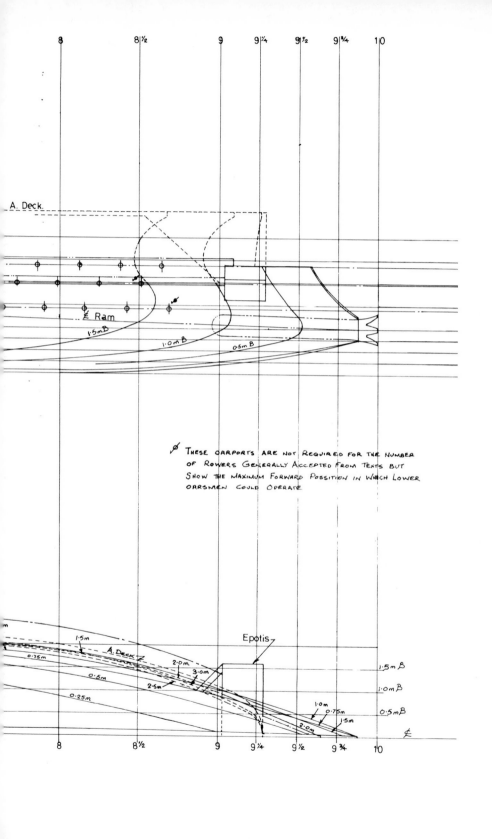

A. Deck.

€ Ram

1·5 m B

1·0 m B

0·5 m B

⌀ THESE OARPORTS ARE NOT REQUIRED FOR THE NUMBER
OF ROWERS GENERALLY ACCEPTED FROM TEXTS BUT
SHOW THE MAXIMUM FORWARD POSSITION IN WHICH LOWER
ORRSMEN COULD OPERATE

1·5m

A. DECK Z

0·75m

0·5m

0·25m

2·0m

3·0m

2·5m

Epotis

1·0m

0·75m

1·5m

2·0m

1·5m B

1·0m B

0·5m B

€

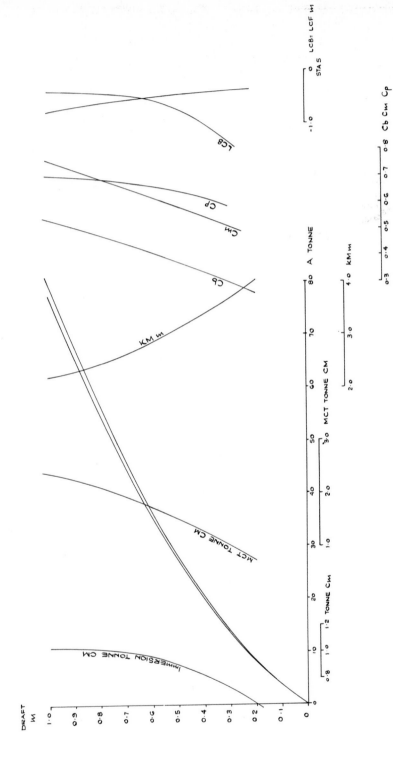

HYDROSTATICS FOR ATHENIAN TRIERES

FIG. 3

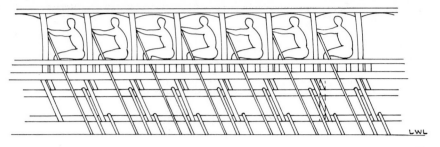

PROFILE INDICATED ON RELIEFS   SCALE ¹/₅₀

FIG. 4

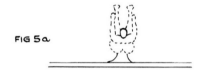

FIG 5a

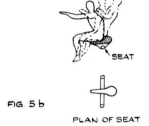

SEAT

FIG. 5 b

PLAN OF SEAT

_____ START OF STROKE

_ _ _ _ _ _ MID STROKE

_ . _ . _ END OF STROKE

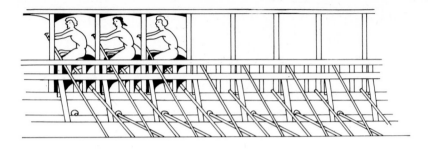

PROFILE AT START OF STROKE

(WITH REVISION FOR PERSPECTIVE)   FIG. 6a

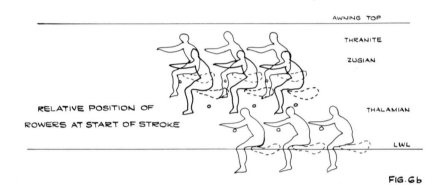

AWNING TOP

THRANITE

ZUGIAN

RELATIVE POSITION OF
ROWERS AT START OF STROKE

THALAMIAN

LWL

FIG. 6b

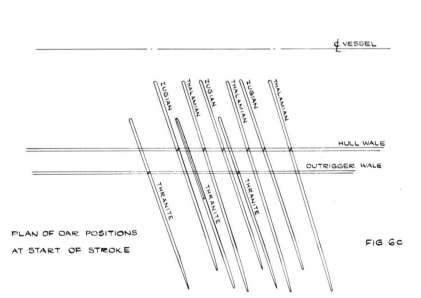

₵ VESSEL

ZUGIAN
THALAMIAN
ZUGIAN
THALAMIAN
ZUGIAN
THALAMIAN

HULL WALE

OUTRIGGER WALE

THRANITE
THRANITE
THRANITE

PLAN OF OAR POSITIONS
AT START OF STROKE

FIG. 6c

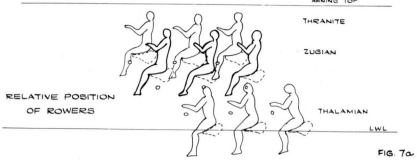

AWNING TOP

THRANITE

ZUGIAN

RELATIVE POSITION
OF ROWERS

THALAMIAN

L W L

FIG. 7a

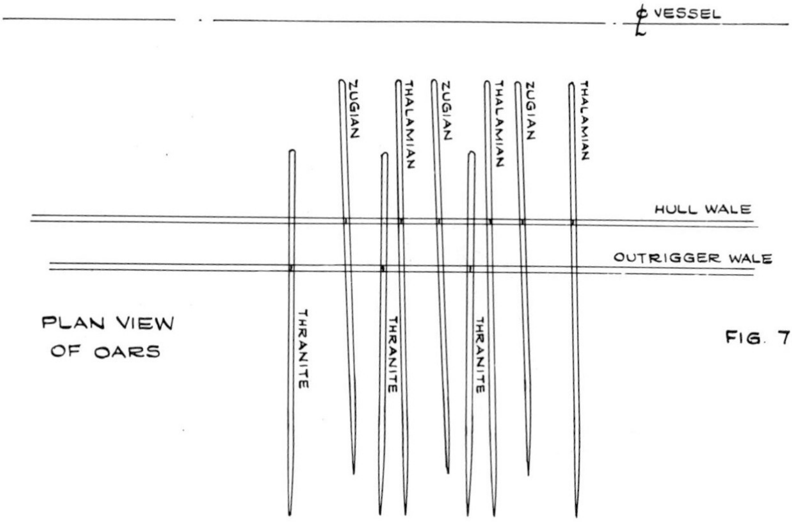

₵ VESSEL

ZUGIAN
THALAMIAN
ZUGIAN
THALAMIAN
ZUGIAN
THALAMIAN

HULL WALE

OUTRIGGER WALE

PLAN VIEW
OF OARS

THRANITE
THRANITE
THRANITE

FIG. 7b

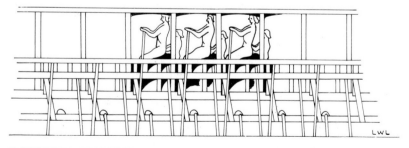

L W L

OUTBOARD PROFILE

FIG. 7c

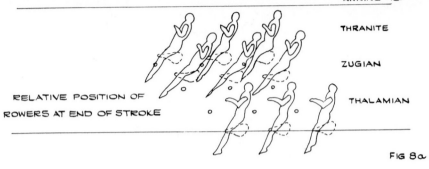

AWNING TOP

THRANITE

ZUGIAN

RELATIVE POSITION OF
ROWERS AT END OF STROKE

THALAMIAN

FIG 8a

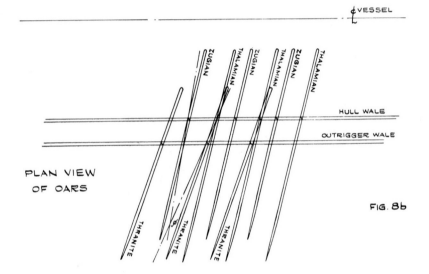

⊄ VESSEL

ZUGIAN

THALAMIAN

ZUGIAN

THALAMIAN

ZUGIAN

THALAMIAN

HULL WALE

OUTRIGGER WALE

PLAN VIEW
OF OARS

THRANITE

THRANITE

THRANITE

FIG. 8b

OUTBOARD PROFILE

FIG. 8c

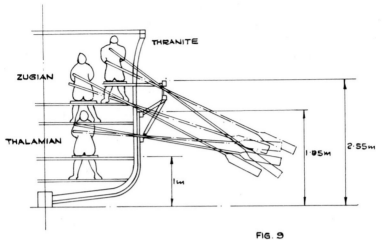

THRANITE

ZUGIAN

THALAMIAN

2·55m

1·85m

1m

FIG. 9

DETAIL OF OUTRIGGER STRUCTURE
BASED UPON CONTEMPORARY ILLUSTRATIONS

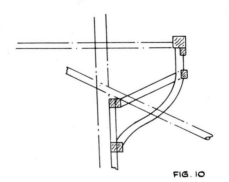

FIG. 10

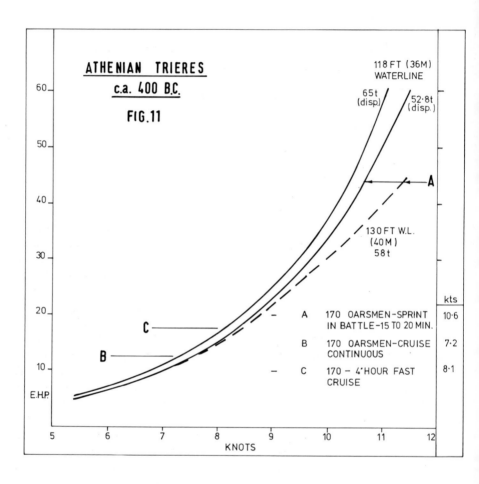

ATHENIAN TRIERES
c.a. 400 B.C.
FIG.11

118 FT (36M) WATERLINE

65t (disp)

52·8t (disp.)

130 FT W.L. (40M) 58t

			kts
A	170 OARSMEN-SPRINT IN BATTLE-15 TO 20 MIN.		10·6
B	170 OARSMEN-CRUISE CONTINUOUS		7·2
C	170 - 4'HOUR FAST CRUISE		8·1

E.H.P.

KNOTS

AN INTRODUCTION: THE DEVELOPMENT OF SCREW
PROPULSION FOR STEAM VESSELS

Basil Greenhill

For mankind as a whole the adoption of steam propulsion at sea was one of the most important and far-reaching developments in modern history. Largely because of Britain's technological, industrial and financial world leadership, which became established in the first half of the last century, this development was from beginning to end principally a British story. Yet this process has not been subjected to rigorous study by modern historians. Most published accounts of the development of steam at sea oversimplify a complex sequence of events. Political, technical, naval and economic historians have all lacked the multi-disciplinary approach necessary for a comprehensive interpretation and explanation of developments which were in part concerned with the minutiae of the mechanics of steam technology and, amongst other things, with the development of lubricants, sealants and the design of bearings as well as the production of metals of uniform quality and at economic cost. These events were concerned also with the economics of merchant ship operation and with the navy's requirements for effective vessels of war. They were concerned too with rapid industrial development ashore, with government financial policy, and with the social and political attitudes of politicians and officials and the deeply entrenched attitudes of seamen.

To simplify, in my turn, there were two problems to be overcome in the development of a steamship capable, as a merchant vessel, of world-wide operation in competition with sailing vessels with their lower investment and operating costs or capable, as a warship, to be an effective instrument of global policy. The first problem was to develop a more efficient means of driving the vessel than the paddle – for the paddle steamer for both merchant shipping and naval purposes was for technical reasons which I have outlined before,[1] a dead end.

Briefly, as a merchant ship, the paddle steamer was limited to short passages or to longer, but still strictly limited, passages with light valuable cargo or passengers. As a warship she could be a tug, a very valuable fast despatch boat – this was perhaps her chief role – or used in reconnaissance and for hydrographic work. Captain Byam Martin summed up the situation very accurately when he wrote in 1854:

I do not anticipate that the command of the paddle steamers can bring much distinction – occasion may arise when they will act in a body and form an important arm of the Fleet; but generally they will be detached in

two's and three's – towing – looking out – and carrying letters ...
Paddlers cannot go into action.[2]

The basic difficulties with the paddler were hydrodynamic. To be efficient she had to be long and narrow. She could not carry big cargoes as a merchant vessel, and her efficiency deteriorated as her draught lessened with the consumption of fuel and the paddles were no longer immersed to their optimum depth. If she was designed, as a warship, to carry heavy guns in her ends – the only place she could carry them – she ceased to be a hydrodynamically efficient steamer. Moreover, the paddle engines, placed high in the vessel, prevented the proper spacing of the masts for sailing if the traditional ship or barque rigs, essential for world-wide sailing, were used as opposed to the schooner type sail-assist rig of the short haul fully-powered steam paddlers like Brunel's *Great Western* of 1837. So, besides being encumbered by her paddles, the placing of her masts made her a poor sailer. In addition, she was, of course, very vulnerable in action, with her machinery and crank shaft far above the water line.

The paddle war vessel really came into her own in the China War of the early 1840s. Steaming up the great rivers, she could demonstrate the power of industrial Britain far inside the coastal boundaries accessible to the sailing warship. In this way the hitherto unbelieving Chinese authorities were slowly convinced of the necessity of co-operation in matters of trade. As the Duke of Wellington wrote in December 1841, success 'depended upon the strength of the means of navigation by steam'.[3]

A more efficient means of propulsion having been achieved, the second problem was to develop a commercially viable marine engine which did not require so much fuel that there was no room left for paying cargo or for guns, ammunition, stores and fighting men.

The first of these problems was overcome in the course of the 1840s by the development of screw propulsion. The solution was the result of close co-operation between the public and private sectors, the Admiralty and the engineering establishment ashore, with the running, on the whole, being made by the private sector, as we would now call it. All this has a surprisingly modern feel about it. The second problem was not solved until the middle 1860s. The answer was provided by the application by the merchant shipping industry of recent industrial and technical developments ashore to produce a commercially viable, economical, marine compound engine with its attendant high pressure boilers.

The two papers which follow deal with the solving of the first of these problems and particularly with the interaction of the Admiralty with the private sector in the 1840s. Greatly expanding on a theme first developed by the late Admiral P.W. Brock and myself in our book *Steam and Sail* in 1973,[4] the papers show that the navy was not, as has so often been alleged by its own historians, dragging its feet in the matter of steam propulsion, but, on the contrary, showed an intense and realistic interest in the development of the screw as a possible way forward from the dead end of the paddle frigate, which they had developed as far as it could then go for their purposes. In the current financial climate the navy was happy for the private sector to initiate research and development but then actually became deeply committed to the screw more rapidly than did the merchant shipping industry, largely because its basic requirements were different.

The two papers also perhaps demonstrate the artificiality of the traditional distinction between naval and merchant shipping history. Here we are dealing with the complex interaction of the navy, merchant shipping, and industry ashore. All are influenced by politics and by international events. Once again we are dealing, not with maritime history but with the maritime aspects of history.

It can be argued that there are two principal reasons why historians have in the past failed to present a proper account of the introduction of steam into the navy. The first has been because they have treated steam propulsion as a continuity, when really it is in two parts. Paddle propulsion and screw propulsion were quite distinct from one another. Historians have perhaps not appreciated the full significance of the dislocation between paddles and screw and the very strict limitations in the uses of the paddle steamer for a Royal Navy which increasingly had to have a world-wide operating range for its line of battleships. Given the technical limitations of steam as already described, until the 1860s world-wide operations could only be conducted under sail. But, if the limitations of the paddle steamer could be overcome, the steam engine could provide auxiliary power to a vessel of war whose prime movers remained the wind and her sails, by giving her great flexibility of movement at close quarters and restricted waters, by making her independent of the weather for short periods of calm, and by greatly increasing her safety in bad weather. Then a new weapon, more truly formidable than anything which had ever existed at sea before, would be created. It was the development of screw propulsion which brought such ships into being, the steam screw battle fleet of the 1850s. Andrew Lambert shows in his paper that, far from delaying the introduction of new technology, as soon as it became practicable to do so the Admiralty developed the effective application of steam power as an auxiliary means of propulsion.

The second reason for the inadequacy of the picture which has often been painted of the history of steam at sea has been the failure to distinguish clearly between the use of steam as the principal means of driving a vessel with auxiliary sails disposed in a schooner rig offering little windage – or sail-assist as such sails and their rigging are now called – and the use of steam in a vessel whose prime means of propulsion remained the wind but which was equipped with a steam engine as an additional occasional source of power. The vessels in the first of these categories can be referred to as fully powered steamships, vessels in the second as auxiliary steamships. For the very practical reasons explained above the navy was not interested in the fully powered steamships, except for the smallest of its vessels. For equally practical reasons the merchant shipping industry was never to be really interested in the auxiliary steamship for general world trade. The advantage gained could never justify financially the investment in auxiliary engines powerful enough to overcome the windage of contemporary sailing vessels' masts and rigging in anything but the lightest of weather, nor could they justify the costs of the necessary additional crew and of fuel.

The commercial practicality of the fully powered steamship operating within a strictly limited range of voyaging, even with the limitations imposed by paddles, had been demonstrated beyond all doubt by the success in the trans-Atlantic passenger trade of the fully-powered *Great Western* of Bristol in the late 1830s (and copies of her logs were duly sent to the very interested Admiralty).[5] Her success led to the building in iron of *The Great Britain* in Bristol in the early 1840s. This vessel, the world's first modern ship, that is, the first big, iron, fully-powered screw driven steamship, conclusively demonstrated the technical and economic practicality of the fully-powered steamship for limited merchant shipping operations. Indeed it can be argued that her stranding in Dundrum Bay in August 1846, when she had already reached a situation of operational profitability delayed the development of the fully-powered merchant steamship by several years. On the other hand, the durability she demonstrated on that occasion probably accelerated the build-up of confidence in iron construction for merchant ships.

Although the Admiralty, with its quite different operational requirements, was concerned with the development of the auxiliary screw steamship, there was much to be learned from the design problems of *The Great Britain* and the operational experience gained with her. As early as November 1840 Captain W. Parry, Controller of Steam Machinery at the Admiralty, was enquiring for details of her hull, machinery and, especially, her screw.[6]

As Andrew Lambert's paper shows, Brunel, the great engineer, as a direct result of his involvement as a major influence in *The Great Britain's* construction, played a very important and continuing part in the design and construction of the *Rattler*, by which the Admiralty gained operational experience which was the basis of the construction, in an astonishingly few years, of the world's first steam screw battle fleet which was to play such a significant part in the coming 'Crimean' War with Russia.[7] The *Rattler* began her long trials in April 1843. *The Great Britain*, which had taken much longer to build, had hers largely on her maiden voyage from Bristol to London two years later, in January 1845. On board her were Commander W. Crispin from the Royal Yacht, a very experienced officer of steamers, and Thomas Lloyd, Inspector of Steam Machinery at Woolwich Dockyard, both of whom reported on the ship's performance to the First Secretary of the Admiralty. Commander Crispin's report has survived and is in most favourable terms.[8]

The paper by myself which follows describes in detail one hitherto unnoticed facet of the interplay of private and public sectors over the development of steam screw propulsion at sea which was taking place at the beginning of the 1840s. Following on this specific example, Andrew Lambert in his paper surveys the whole scene and convincingly demonstrates the Admiralty's deep practical involvement with the advancement of steam technology. He also clarifies the role of Brunel, which was altogether more positive than some previous writers have suggested. Andrew Lambert's work has also cast much new light on the historic significance of *The Great Britain* and it is appropriate that it should have been sponsored by the S.S. Great Britain Project in Bristol, the body responsible for the restoration of this vessel to her 1844 glory, now well on its way to completion, in the dock in which she was built.

It is also appropriate that Dr Ewan Corlett, who more than anyone else was responsible for the return of *The Great Britain* to this country, should have taken the chair at the presentation of these two papers at Dartington and should have proposed in his summing up that an interdisciplinary team should be set up to further the study in depth, in its many ramifications, of the introduction of steam, and especially of screw propulsion, at sea. This, to reiterate, was one of mankind's great steps forward. It would be right and proper that the University of Exeter, which in recent years has so clearly and practically recognised the significance of the maritime aspects of historical studies, should take this very important project under its wing.

NOTES

1   Basil Greenhill and Ann Giffard, *The British Assault on Finland* (London, 1988), 66-70; P.W. Brock and Basil Greenhill, *Steam and Sail* (Newton Abbot, 1973), 11, 12.

2   National Maritime Museum, J.O.D. 200/1 and 2; Byam Martin, *Baltic Journal* (1854).

3   Wellington Papers; Wellington to Ellenborough, 29 December 1841, quoted in G.S. Graham, *The China Station* (Oxford, 1978), 196.

4   Brock and Greenhill, *Steam and Sail*, 10, 11, 12, 14.

5   Parry to Claxton, 12 July 1838, PRO, ADM 92/4, 236.

6   Parry to Claxton, 6 November 1840, PRO, ADM 94/4, 420-1.

7   Greenhill and Giffard, *British Assault on Finland*; A.D. Lambert, *Battleships in Transition. The Creation of the Steam Battlefleet, 1815-1860* (London, 1983), 41-52.

8   Crispin to Herbert, 29 November 1845, PRO, ADM 87/15, S3458.

THE SCREW STEAMSHIP *GREAT NORTHERN*

Basil Greenhill

This paper arises from a casual examination of the appendices to Murray's *Rudimentary Treatise on Marine Engines and Steam Vessels*, of 1852,[1] which revealed the listing among merchant screw steamships then afloat of a vessel named the *Great Northern* which had a larger tonnage than any other vessel on the list except *The Great Britain*. This matter clearly merited investigation.[2]

Research revealed that the *Great Northern* was the largest screw propelled merchant steamship in the world at the time of her launch in July 1842, and the first steamship to have her machinery and boilers placed in the after part of the vessel. She had forty ports for eighteen-pounder guns and in conception at least, can be thought of as the first screw frigate. She appears to have been fitted with a lifting screw to be raised when the vessel was under sail. Francis Pettit Smith, the British pioneer and promoter of screw propulsion, was very closely associated with her construction. After the floating out of *The Great Britain* in 1843 she remained the second largest screw steamship in the world until the beginning of the building of the steam screw battle fleet at the end of the 1840s and the launch of the iron *City of Glasgow* in 1850. Her short career casts some new light on the interaction of the Admiralty and the private sector at this period of intense experimental interest in the development of screw propulsion. On the frontiers of the technological development of her period she represented a very daring and original entrepreneurial venture. Not surprisingly, perhaps, like some of her contemporary smaller-scale experiments with screw propulsion[3] she was not a commercial success and her backers, but not, apparently, her builder, lost money on the enterprise.

The first reference to Captain William Coppin, the builder of the *Great Northern*, I have so far been able to trace is in Esther Clark Wright's, *Saint John Ships and their Builders*.[4] Here he is recorded as the builder of the brigantine *Kathleen* in New Brunswick in 1829 and subsequently as the master of the ship *Prudence* built by John Smith at Portland, New Brunswick, in 1832, for Matthew Delap. This vessel made one passage, to Londonderry in 1832, where she was sold to J. Kelso and Company of that town. According to the late Ernest B. Anderson, Captain Coppin based himself in Londonderry and soon became established as a builder, not only of merchant sailing vessels but also of paddle steamers for Irish Sea packet routes.[5] According to the *Shipping and Mercantile Gazette*[6] these included the *Maiden City*, completed in 1842 for service between London and Liverpool. Anderson's account of the genesis of the *Great Northern* is as follows:

when screw propulsion first came out, Captain Coppin immediately interested himself in it and started to build the largest vessel at that time yet to be seen, also undertaking the building of the engines and boilers himself. She was called the Great Northern .... [7]

This enterprising Canadian was already, in 1839, the subject of a laudatory poem of 98 verses entitled "An Original Poem on the Merits of Captain Coppin and the Enterprising Spirit he has so Nobly Manifested by his Introduction of Grand Machinery for Purposes of Shipbuilding &c", by R. Taggart, published as a pamphlet.[8] It begins:

Hail! Captain Coppin, Neptune's brightest star, That shines with splendour and effulgence bright.

and it continues prophetically:

He'll build fine ships, of great enormous size.

This Captain Coppin was certainly to do.

The first documentary reference to the *Great Northern* I have so far been able to trace is an item in the *Londonderry Standard* of March 1842[9] to the effect that:

During the past week Mr. F.P. Smith, the patentee of the Archimedes screw propeller, visited this City to supervise the installation of his invention in the large vessel now being built by Captain Coppin. Smith said he was very satisfied with Coppin's vessel. The ship is double ceiled, diagonally from bilge to gunwhale with planks crossing each other at right angles. The longitudinal fastenings of her decks, with iron knees, are screw bolted through, forming one solid mass of wood and iron. Her engines and boilers, fast progressing in the same yard, will occupy only about $1/_6$th of her hold, leaving sufficient room for 1300 tons of cargo, with about 700 tons of coal, and an entire deck free for the accommodation of passengers. She will be fully ship rigged and have the appearance of a frigate, being pierced for 44 guns on her upper deck. With her lovely entrance and run we think she will be one of the fastest ships afloat. She would make an excellent troop ship for the East Indies. She will have many advantages which no vessel of her tonnage can as yet boast of – in being able to combine the velocity she will acquire by the screw propeller, with that of her sails, she will be able to make very short passages, and having been built on a completely new principle she will carry a large cargo on a very light draught of water.

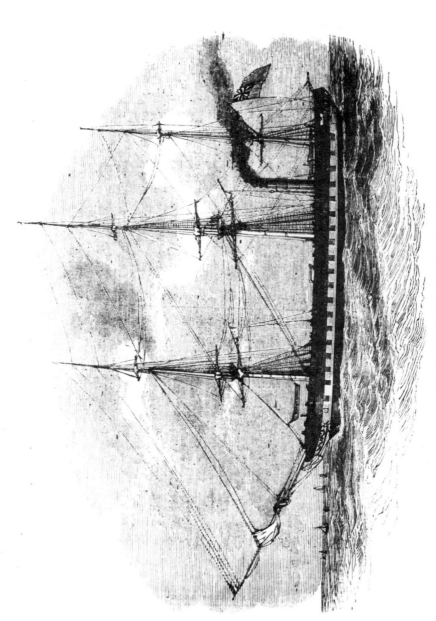

The Great Northern under Steam

(Illustrated London News)

The next evidence for the existence of the *Great Northern* appears to be an instruction to the Surveyor of the Navy, Sir William Symonds, from Sir John Barrow, Second Secretary to the Admiralty, dated 3 May 1862, as follows:

You are to send one of the Dock Yard Officers to Derry to examine a large vessel lately built there for the purpose of sailing and steaming, and which has been offered to the Admiralty, either to purchase, or to hire as a Transport. The Officer is to ascertain whether her scantling, her Beams and her Decks are such as would admit of heavy guns being placed in her; what amount of complement she could conveniently carry, if fitted as a ship of War, – the masts and yards, – the power and apparent efficiency of her Engines for propelling her – and the number of days' fuel she can carry. Also supposing her to be unfit for a vessel of War, what description of Accommodation she can afford for Troops or Passengers, and for what number of either. With such other remarks respecting the vessel as may enable their Lordships to decide whether it be desirable to enter into negotiations with the Owners regarding her.[10]

This is followed by a report from William Blessley, Foreman of Sheerness Dockyard, and an official of great experience whose record and subsequent career shows that he was held in high respect, to Symonds, dated Londonderry, 10 May 1842.[11] Blessley begins:

I have been to Londonderry and surveyed a steam vessel in building at that place for the purpose of sailing and steaming and which has been offered to the Admiralty either to purchase or hire as a transport. To which I beg to state that she is constructed for a Sailing Ship as well as a Steamer, propelled by a Smith's Patent Screw, which is fitted in her after deadwood being 7 feet long and 11 feet diameter, with her Engines, Boilers and Coal Boxes, for about 400 tons of Coals, in her After part. The whole occupying about $\frac{1}{6}$ of the vessel's capacity. She is of good capacity, carefully put together and well Caulked. The greater part of her Frame is of British Oak <u>having her Beams, Shelves, Waterways, Decks, and the greater part of her Planking made out of Fir.</u> She has 22 Ports on each side of her Spar Deck for Broadside Guns, <u>but the Topside is not of sufficient strength for carrying them</u> ... she is supposed to be ready for launching in about three or four weeks, and her Engines &c complete in about 10 weeks from this date, and <u>the only objectionable part of her fastenings is the iron Keelson Bolts.</u>

(The underlined passages above are marked in red in the original document).

This letter was accompanied by a Surveyor's Report, made on 7 May 1842, which gave further particulars of the vessel in more detail. She was to have two 'Marine Condensing Engines of 364 Combined Horses Power of 68 inches diameter

Cylinder and 4 foot 6 inch Stroke ... the Boilers are Circular, in 3 distinct parts with 4 Furnaces to each, and placed in the After part of the vessel'. Her dimensions were 218 feet 10 inches from the foreside of the stem to the afterside of the stern post at the height of the upper deck, her extreme breadth on wales was 36 feet 9 inches and her depth of hold 18 feet 6 inches. Her tonnage by the old rule was 1388 92/94ths, by the Act of 1835 1360 76/350ths. Further notes in the report show that 20 of the floors were of rock elm, the rest of British oak. The rest of the constituent parts of the frames were of British oak, except that every alternate top timber was of British larch. Her decks were of red pine and yellow pine and she was fastened with double treenails and iron butt bolts. The vessel had been built to the draught of Mr. Coppin and on speculation.

In his covering minute submitting this report to the Admiralty Board Sir William Symonds commented:[12]

From Mr. Blessley's report she appears strongly put together, and that she is very capacious as to room; But I fear that some of her materials are of doubtful durability which I have marked in his report with Red Ink.

The vessel described in the foregoing paragraphs must be of considerable interest in the history of the screw propelled steamship. In fact the *Great Northern* was pressing on the upper limits of size possible with wooden construction using the techniques of the very early 1840s. Though the subject invites further detailed research it seems likely that the building of the much larger wooden merchant paddle steamers and sailing vessels which was to follow on both sides of the Atlantic in the later 1840s and early 1850s was made possible by the use of iron diagonal strap bracing let into the outer surfaces of the frames under the planking.[13] This method of strengthening was still in use in the six-master schooner *Wyoming*, of 1909, the largest wooden sailing vessel ever to earn her living at sea.[14]

There is little evidence as to the decision-making process which led to the construction of the *Great Northern*. Her conception was, of course, very different from that of *The Great Britain*. The latter was a fully-powered iron steamship with very sophisticated sail assist. The *Great Northern* was the first large steam screw auxiliary sailing vessel and the first powered vessel to follow a practice now almost universal and have her 'machinery aft', in the words subsequently to be used of such vessels in the description in Lloyd's Register. Given that in the two years preceding her construction the Ship Propeller Company had been parading their experimental screw steamship *Archimedes* around the British Isles in a vigorous promotion and sales campaign for Francis Pettit Smith's screw propeller placed between the stern posts and the rudder,[15] and given that the *Great Northern* was fitted with her propeller in the position covered by Smith's patent, and that Smith himself clearly showed great interest in her construction and subsequent trials, it seems permissible to postulate that the enterprising Canadian, William Coppin, embarked on her construction, hazarding large sums of local capital, in the belief that there was a reasonable chance of getting in on the lowest part of the ground floor of a great new commercial development with a lucrative Admiralty charter or sale. He may have figured (to use the Canadian expression) that the high risk was really limited to the capital invested in the machinery, since the ship, if too far ahead of her time as an auxiliary, would always find a ready market as a sailing vessel.

At the beginning of the 1840s no naval vessel larger than a brig had been commissioned from a private yard since the end of the Napoleonic Wars in 1815. William Coppin may well have thought that in the new and experimental situation created by the development of screw propulsion the Admiralty would be ready to vary its policy of commissioning large vessels built only in the royal dockyards and make use of vessels purchased from the private sector. If so, he was disastrously wrong. The Admiralty were happy for the private sector to make the running and to a degree to work with the private sector, as is evinced by their interest in the *Archimedes* and *The Great Britain* and their readiness to work with Brunel with whom they had already been deeply involved for more than a year at the time of the launch of the *Great Northern*, as is revealed in Andrew Lambert's paper. Their own experimental vessel was going to be the *Rattler*, developed and built to an Admiralty specification, and not a merchant-yard-built vessel which, however well constructed, included doubtful materials in her fabric and which was equipped with an engine of uncertain design and quality. It can also be argued that William Coppin was too late, for the *Rattler* was already under construction when the *Great Northern* was launched.[16]

On 23 July 1842 the *Northern Whig*[17] reported that the vessel was nearly ready for launching and on 27 July the *Londonderry Standard*[18] reported in ecstatic terms that the launch had actually taken place on 23 July in the presence of at least 20,000 spectators gathered, according to the *Northern Whig*'s subsequent account of the event, from England and Scotland as well as from all over Ireland. The *Londonderry Standard*'s account of the launch contains information about the screw and propelling machinery, which, since it may well, from its detail, have been derived from a handout from the Ship Propeller Company, is worth recording in full:

> She is to be propelled by Smith's Archimedean screw, which will be 12 feet diameter and 14 feet pitch, but the length will only be 7 feet. It is to make 88 revolutions per minute. The gearing consists of a cog-wheel, 20 feet diameter, working into a smaller wheel 5 feet diameter, upon whose axis is the shaft of the screw. The engine power consists of 2 cylinders, 68 inches in diameter, 4 feet 6 inches stroke, and to make 22 strokes per minute; nominal power above 370 horses; there are to be 4 air pumps, 19 inches diameter, and 4 feet 6 inches stroke, and cylindrical boilers. The engines are to be placed close abaft the vessel leaving the midships clear for passengers.

In its issue of 12 October 1842[19] the *Londonderry Standard* was to be more specific about the placing of the screw, stating that the *Great Northern* was:

48

to be propelled by Smith's Screw Propeller, which is fitted in a space left for the purpose in the deadwood abaft. The screw is 11 feet diameter, and 14 feet pitch, and is intended to make 88 revolutions per minute. The screw is driven by a pair of engines with a collective power of 360 horsepower, working at a pressure of 3 lbs. to the inch.

On 13 August 1842 the *Great Northern* was registered as No. 4 of that year of Londonderry. Her builder's certificate was signed by William Coppin on 30 July. She was registered as owned 32/64ths each by Joseph Kelso and Robert Lyons, merchants of Londonderry. A transcript of her Londonderry registration is appended to this paper. It is to be noted that there are variations between the measurements for statutory registration and those of William Blessley, the Admiralty Surveyor.

Fitting out and rigging proceeded in Londonderry. On 23 November 1842 the *Londonderry Standard*[20] reported that she had sailed on November 21, 'to go to the deep water anchorage at Moville, then to go to Southampton to be surveyed by the Admiralty ... going over the shallows [in the River Foyle] the *Great Northern* made 7 knots per hour, but she got up to 8 knots per hour [10 mph] before she anchored in deep water off Moville. It is only just to believe that she will sail [that is, she will steam] at the rate of 9 or 10 knots per hour because at no time during the trip did the screw make more than 15 revolutions per minute out of the 22 which it was calculated to make, only 2/3 of the proper steam power being applied'.

On 28 December 1842 the *Londonderry Standard*[21] reported that the vessel had left Moville on December 17 bound for England – 'stormy winds and fog for most of the voyage. Made Isle of Wight on 22nd December, but did not anchor at Cowes until 23rd December. During the last two days she made fully 2/3 of her voyage and in speed far exceeded the expectation of her builder. Steam power was only used for about 18 hours.' Very significantly, the Lloyd's report of her arrival at Cowes states her as having come in 'to repair engine'.

Extracts from the *Great Northern*'s log book on her passage from Cowes to London,[22] as transmitted to the Admiralty from Francis Pettit Smith, show that the vessel was operated much as auxiliary steamships were to be sailed for the next hundred years. On 25 December 1842, she steamed as far as the Owers Light where they 'Stopped Engines ... and disconnected the Screw'. It is thus apparent that this first large screw-propelled steamship had some kind of sailing clutch. She then proceeded under sail only as far as the Downs, where she lay at anchor in a gale from the west south west and had to send down royal and topgallant yards. She lay in the Downs all December 26, and, the weather moderating on the following morning, the log records, '10.20 a.m. Steam raised to assist in getting the anchor. 11.40 a.m. Got under way and proceeded through the Downs setting fore and aft sails the meantime. 2.30 a.m. Abreast of Margate. Took in all sail wind being directly ahead. 4.20 p.m. Abreast of the Mouse Light. Rate of 7 knots per Masseys Log'. She anchored abreast of the Chapman Beacon and on the morning of 28 December steamed up the Thames against the ebb as far as Blackwall. The next day she steamed into the East India Import Dock.

There is a most interesting minute written in the margins of the above-quoted extracts from the Log as the paper lies in the Public Record Office today. This reads:

Sir Geo. Cockburn, 31st December, 1842, submitted that Captain Supt. Fras Collier be directed to send Lloyd to meet me on board the 'Great Northern' in the East India Import Dock on Tuesday next at 1/2 12. The card of admission to be forwarded. W. Parry. Directions accordingly.

Admiral Sir George Cockburn was, of course, the First Naval Lord, Captain Francis Collier was the Superintendent of Woolwich Dockyard, Thomas Lloyd was the brilliant Inspector of Steam Machinery at Woolwich who was to move on to become Engineer in Chief of the Navy and a Companion of the Bath, and of whom it was to be written by the then Controller of the Navy, at the time of Lloyd's retirement in 1869 that:[23]

To Mr. Lloyd, more than anyone else, is due the successful application of the screw to the propulsion of steamships, and it was owing to his enlightened knowledge and his zealous exertions that the Royal Navy was enabled to take the lead in its application to ships of War.

W. Parry was Captain W. E. Parry, Controller of Steam Machinery. At this time one of Parry's duties was to protect the Admiralty Board from the 'host of speculative inventors' who were one of the phenomena of this period of very rapid and revolutionary technical development, 'selecting from the many inventions the few that have merit' for trial at Woolwich.[24] It is apparent therefore that the *Great Northern* was being taken very seriously by the principal Admiralty officials concerned with the development of steam propulsion.

On 14 January the *Illustrated London News* reported the presence of the *Great Northern* in London, stating that, 'This extraordinary steamer, now in the East India Docks, is the object of general astonishment ... During the week many persons entered the Dockyard to gaze at this really wonderful object'.[25] The accompanying drawings, reproduced here, purport to give details of the arrangement of the screw and a profile of the vessel herself. From these drawings it would appear that the vessel was equipped with a lifting screw in a trunk. If so, in this way also, she was a pioneer of much that was to follow.

Nevertheless she was to lie in London Dock for most of the rest of her life. Allowing for London prejudice against vessels built elsewhere than on the Thames, nevertheless some hint of what was wrong can perhaps be gained from an article in *The Artizan* of January, 1843.[26] The criticism was of the engines:

Never in any steam vessel, did we see engines so badly planned, or so badly constructed. There are two engines, standing one before the other, and situated in the stern part of the ship: the cranks are immediately over

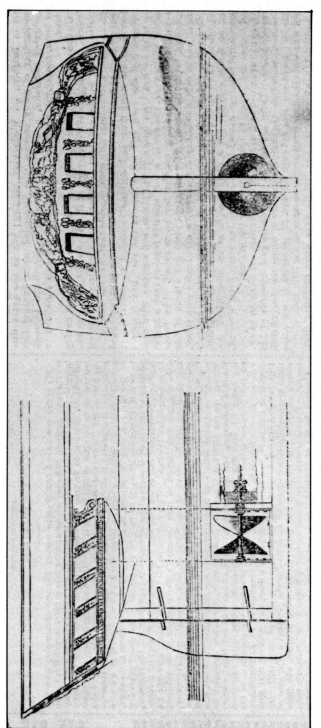

Stern of the Great Northern showing the aperture specified by F.P. Smith for the screw. There is an indication also of the trunk for lifting the screw when under sail. (Illustrated London News)

the cylinders; and on the intermediate shaft, which is of course parallel to the keel, a great cogwheel, 20 feet in diameter, is placed, which works in a pinion below, situated on the shaft which gives motion to the screw. The crank is not joined to the piston rod by means of a connecting rod, but a frame is attached to the piston rod top, with a great transverse slot for the crank pin to work in; and as the piston rod moves up, the crank pin moves in this slot, so as to accommodate itself to the piston's altered position: the movement of this frame is restricted to the perpendicular position by strong guides.

There is nothing original in this plan and much that is bad. The friction is enormous; the wear of the parts rapid; and the difficulty of adjustment considerable. The horizontal groove in which the crank pin works, it is impossible, we understand, to keep from heating; of which indeed, the iron of the frame bears evidence – its edges being frayed, and its surface rendered irregular, by the enormous pressure of the travelling crank pins. The crank pin may, indeed, be encircled by a friction roller to mitigate these evils, but this is a futile expedient: the roller must speedily wear a little flat on the one side, and after that it will never turn round.

Other faults – a vast complication of pipes in the lower regions of the engine house. The mode of throwing the eccentric rod up out of gear, consists in the application of a rope and pulleys; the upper end of which is attached to the deck and with which the Engineer hauls the rod bodily out of the notch. The starting lever consists of an immense bar, heavy enough to form the beam of a small engine; and which, before it can be detached from the engine, must be lifted in toto from its place; an operation of course impossible when the engine is at work. This bar must therefore be in perpetual motion after the engine is set on, and must constitute a source of much danger to the engineer.

We cannot believe that any drawings of the engine were made previous to their construction. The whole is thrown together as if by chance.

The article went on to describe the screw as '11 feet in diameter, set to the pitch of 14 feet, consists of two half turns or threads, which makes it 7 feet in length and makes 4 revolutions for the one at the engine'.

In assessing *The Artizan*'s report it must be remembered that before the *Great Northern* no big engine had been built to drive a screw propeller at sea. Indeed it was probably beyond the technology of the late 1830s to do so. Even Brunel had sidestepped the problem with the solution for *The Great Britain* of an adaption of a paddle propulsion unit designed by his father which gave good and commercially viable service until it was ruined by a winter on the beach after the vessel had grounded in Dundrum Bay. It is by no means surprising that a journalist, who may well have been under instruction to find fault with this non-river built pioneer, could find much to criticise. Nevertheless the *Great Northern*'s career suggests that there was something fundamentally wrong with these experimental engines designed and constructed in William Coppin's shipyard.

Whatever the truth of *The Artizan*'s comments the *Great Northern* spent much of 1843 lying in London Docks having modifications made to her engines. According to an article in the *London Journal of Commerce*[27] they had been assembled originally from parts made in Liverpool, in Scotland and in Londonderry. The modifications were made by Messrs. Miller and Ravenhill, engineers of considerable repute and with much experience of marine work, at a reported cost of £4,000.[28] Henceforth the engines appeared to have been spoken of as 'by Miller and Ravenhill'.

In August it was reported[29] that she was to make an 'experimental trip soon to try her improved engines, then she will go on a voyage to Calcutta, and a great number of private and state cabins are being fitted up for families'. On 20 September 1843 the vessel was registered anew as of London with owners Robert Lyons now of Poplar, Middlesex, shipowner, and Joseph Kelso of Londonderry.[30] The experimental trip, which was in fact evidently intended to be a further sales demonstration trip for the Admiralty, took place on 11 October 1843, and was from Blackwall to Greenhythe and back, with Mr. Miller himself in charge of the engines. The *London Journal of Commerce* reported what happened:[31]

The tide was against her on the trip out. A very powerful vessel. The advantages of the screw propeller over paddles, engine working at 19 strokes per minute, Mr. Miller, the ship's Engineer, must be applauded for getting such performance from an engine that is made up of different pieces .... The *Great Northern*'s steam engine is intended to be auxiliary. On her trip she steamed at 7 1/2 knots an hour against the tide, which was 2 1/2 knots against her, making her steaming 10 knots an hour through the water. The log gave a statute mile in 8 minutes 2 seconds when the vessel was off Erith, which equals 9 minutes 12 seconds for a nautical mile.

Captain Sir Francis Collier, Thomas Lloyd, Francis Pettit Smith and Captain Chapell, an officer who was deeply involved with Parry over the development of the screw, were all on board the *Great Northern* on this sales trip. But it was to be of no avail. The next evidence of her fate is in a letter to Sir Sydney Herbert, then Secretary to the Admiralty, dated 21 November 1843, from a shipbroker, I.M. Sunley of 71, Cornhill, which read:[32]

Sir

The owners of the steamship *Great Northern* have requested me to tender her for sale to the Lords Commissioners of H.M. Navy under the conviction that she is eminently adapted for the Service.

The large expenditure which has been incurred in the building and completion of this superior ship has so crippled the finances of the owners that they would prefer selling it at a very considerable sacrifice of cost to sailing her on their own account as they originally intended.

The engines are in the most perfect working order and just from the hands of Messrs. Miller and Ravenhill. As regards the ship, I will merely say that all the scientific who have inspected her have expressed their admiration of her great strength of the perfection of her construction. Should Their Lordships entertain this proposition I will submit the terms and particulars, it will then be apparent to Their Lordships how great a sacrifice is offered to their consideration.

A minute of the following day reads: 'Thank him but I have no intention of purchasing this vessel'.

The Artizan formerly withdrew its objections to the vessel and apologised 'for the ferocity of our earlier comments on the Great Northern. We can now praise her because the owners have removed most of the evils of which we complained. The alterations in the machinery do much credit to Messrs. Miller and Ravenhill, by whom they were accomplished and the Great Northern is now an efficient serviceable vessel, and we may add a marketable one'.[33]

On 7 June 1845 an advertisement appeared in the Shipping and Mercantile Gazette[34] stating that the fine frigate-built steamship Great Northern was to be sold at auction at Lloyd's Captain Room, Royal Exchange on June 26th by order of the mortgagees. No change of ownership is noted on the Register and there is no other mention of the Great Northern in the Shipping and Mercantile Gazette in 1845. There is no evidence that the auction actually ever took place or, if it did, that a sum satisfactory to the mortgagees was offered for the vessel.

A search kindly undertaken by Dr Jamieson of the Custom's bills of entry for London, Liverpool, Bristol and Hull from 1843 to 1848 inclusive, and also the crew agreements for the Port of London from 1844 to 1849 inclusive,[35] has produced no reference to the Great Northern. Prof. Fischer has also kindly done the same at the Memorial University of Newfoundland and has also checked Lloyd's lists. No reference to any movement by the Great Northern has been found nor has any further reference to her been found in any of the contemporary shipping journals which Dr Jamieson was also kind enough to search. It must be assumed that she never again left London River, though why she was not sold for operation as a sailing vessel remains a mystery, since she appears to have been of a construction superior to many merchant vessels of her period and William Coppin's reputation as a builder was very good.

The final documentary reference to the Great Northern appears to be in a note added to her London Registration document of September 1843, 'Certificate cancelled 16.9.51 vessel having been broken up', and then in pencil underneath the footnote: 'Sold to Mr. Beech of Rotherhythe, Surrey and broken up. Beech last owner'.

Anderson records that after the sale of the Great Northern William Coppin built another larger steamer which was, however, destroyed by fire in 1846 before she was launched.[36] He gave up shipbuilding, but continued in business with an engineering works and iron foundry and as a shipowner until 1870. He was a successful salvage engineer, being involved in the saving of 140 vessels. His shipowning activities included the operation of his paddle steamer Ardentinnie as a blockade runner during the American Civil War. Sholto Cooke in his book The

Maiden City and the Western Ocean[37] noted, in a very brief account of William Coppin's career, that his backers, especially Joseph Kelso, suffered heavily for supporting Coppin. It is to be noted that in the registrations of the *Great Northern* there is no evidence of Coppin's direct financial involvement in the venture. It seems therefore that the enterprising Canadian himself avoided the financial disaster which followed his great pioneering venture.

APPENDIX

No. Four, Port Londonderry dated 13th August 1842

Name: Great Northern Burthen 1111 $\frac{60}{100}$ Tons

Christopher Forrest Master

Remeasured under Act. 1430 Tons

Built at Londonderry, in the County of Londonderry in the present year One Thousand and Eight Hundred and Forty Two, as appears by the Certificate of William Coppin, the builder dated at Londonderry 30th July, 1842.

Thomas Dysart,
The Surveying Officer

Two Decks, Three Masts, Length 217 feet.
Taken in Midships Breadth 33 feet.
Depth in Hold 26 feet two tenths.
Propelled by Steam Engine Room 73 feet.
Ship rigged with a standing Bowsprit.
Square sterned, Carvel built, False galleries, Female Figure Head.
And measured on the Stocks.

SUBSCRIBING OWNERS

Joseph Kelso of the City of Londonderry   Merchant.
Robert Lyons of the Said City   Merchant.

OTHER OWNERS

NONE

Custom House 23 August 1842

Joseph Kelso of the City of Londonderry Merchant owner of 32/64 shares, and Robert Lyons of said City Owner of 32/64 shares of said Vessel "Great Northern" have by way of assignment of Mortgage Folio transferred and made over the aforesaid steamship "Great Northern" with her tackle and engines to JOSEPH SOMES Esq. of BROAD STREET, RATCLIFF, in the County of Middlesex, Shipowner. Security for the payment of the sum of £5,000 lent by the said Joseph Somes to Robert Kelso and Robert Lyons, with all interest specified. In failure of said Mortgages the whole of said vessel to become the undisputed property of Joseph Kelso of the City of Londonderry Merchant Owner of 32/64 shares of the above ships and Robert Lyons of the said City the Owner of the other 32/64 shares of the same ship transferred by deed of Mortgage dated 3rd June, 1843, 64/64 shares of the said ship to JOHN MALTBY SUNLEY, of Cornhill in the City of London, Ship and Insurance Agent, to secure certain money therein mentioned not exceeding in the whole £5,850 subject to the before mentioned assignment by way of Mortgage to Joseph SOMES Esq. dated 23rd August, 1842.

(Recorded) Custom House Derry 8th June 1843

There are no further entries in the Register.

NOTES

1   Murray, *Rudimentary Treatise on Marine Engines and Steam Vessels, etc* (London, 1852), 202.

2   While in the later stages of work on Basil Greenhill and Ann Giffard, *The British Assault on Finland* (London, 1988) I had occasion to check Murray's Table 4 on p. 202, The Principal Dimensions of Twenty-Eight Merchant Steamers with Screw Propellers. This revealed the existence of the *Great Northern* with a higher tonnage at 1750, old builder's measurement, than any other vessel on the list except *The Great Britain*. By strange coincidence a week or two later Malcolm Darch of Salcombe mentioned to me that a large

wooden steamship had been launched in Londonderry a year before *The Great Britain* was floated out of her building dock. A xerox of a page of the *Illustrated London News* showed this vessel to have been the *Great Northern*. The vessel has not attracted the attention of historians. Apart from Murray, she is mentioned in Lt. W. Gordon, R.N., *The Economy of the Maritime Steam Engine* (London, 1845), as 'the largest vessel, except the *Great Britain*, to which the screw propeller has been hitherto applied'. This reference is followed by particulars of the vessel. It appears that the only other history of marine engineering or of the steam vessel to mention her is E. Smith, *A Short History of Naval and Marine Engineering* (Cambridge, 1937). None of the modern books purporting to give a history of the origins of steam propulsion at sea mentions her.

The paper on this vessel which follows could not have been prepared without the enthusiastic assistance of Dr Alan Jamieson to whom I am most grateful, as I am to Dr Andrew Lambert. Professor Lewis Fischer, Robin Craig and James Richard, who provided most valuable references, have also been extremely helpful,as has Dr Philip Ollerenshaw of Bristol and Michael Macauglan of the Ulster Folk and Transport Museum.

3   See, for instance, Martin and McCord, 'The Steamship *Bedlington*, 1841-54', in *Maritime History*, 1, 1 (1971), 46-64.

4   Esther Clark Wright, *Saint John Ships and their Builders* (Wolfville, Nova Scotia, 1975), 70, 175.

5   Ernest B. Anderson, *Sailing Ships of Ireland* (Dublin, c. 1958), 246-9.

6   *Shipping and Mercantile Gazette*, London, 4 January 1843. Anderson, *Sailing Ships*, 24 also ascribes to Coppin the building of the paddle steamers *City of Derry* and *Wm. McCormick* for the North West of Ireland Steamship Co. and the *Lady Franklin, Lion* and the *Ardentinnie* for operation under his own management.

7   Anderson, *Sailing Ships*, 247.

8   R. Taggart, *An Original Poem on the Merits of Captain Coppin* (Derry, 1839), verses 1 and 3.

9   *Londonderry Standard*, 23 March 1842.

10 Barrow to Symonds, 3 May 1842, PRO, ADM/1, 5522, 3143.

11 Blessley to Symonds, 9 May 1842, PRO, ADM/1, 5522, S 3226.

12 Symonds to Admiralty, 13 May 1842, PRO, ADM/1 5522, No. 397.

13　D. MacGregor, *Merchant Sailing Ships, 1850-75* (London, 1984), 46-7.

14　W.J. Lewis Parker, *The Great Coal Schooners of New England* (Mystic, Connecticut, 1948), 83-4; H. Underhill, *Deep Water Sail* (Glasgow, 1963), 235-6.

15　The events leading to the general adoption of the screw propeller at sea have been narrated many times, often not by any means accurately, but there has been little modern published work from primary sources. To date the best brief summary has been in Ewan Corlett, *The Iron Ship* (Bradford on Avon, 1983), Chap. 6. To some extent this chapter will now require amendment in the light of this paper and that of Dr. Lambert which follows. See also A. Lambert, *Battleships in Transition* (London, 1984); R. Craig, *Steam Tramps and Cargo Liners* (London, 1980); E. Smith, *A Short History of Naval and Marine Engineering* (Cambridge, 1937); and Greenhill and Giffard, *British Assault on Finland*.

16　The extent of contemporary interest in the possibilities of screw propulsion is shown by the number of vessels, with screws fitted in accordance with F.P. Smith's patent, built in the early 1840s. According to the *Londonderry Standard* of 27 June 1842 besides the huge *The Great Britain* and the *Rattler*, both under construction at the time the *Great Northern* was launched, and the *Archimedes*, there were already in service the *Bedlington* (270 tons, 60 H.P.), the *Princess Royal* (101 tons, 45 H.P.), the little *Bee* (30 tons, 10 H.P.), and the auxiliary *Novelty* (300 tons, 25 H.P.). The latter vessel took 420 tons of cargo from Liverpool to Constantinople in the early 1840s. In addition to these vessels two packets for the French post office service and the French warship *L'Orient* had screws placed as patented by Smith. Part of this list also appeared in the *Nautical Magazine*, XI (1842), 850, and in the *Shipping Gazette* of 9 December 1842 and the source may well have been The Ship Propeller Company itself. See also Martin and McCord, 'Steamship *Bedlington*'.

17　*Northern Whig*, 23 July 1842.

18　*Londonderry Standard*, 27 July 1842.

19　*Londonderry Standard*, 12 October 1842.

20　*Londonderry Standard*, 23 November 1842.

21　*Londonderry Standard*, 28 December 1842.

22　From "Mr. Smith, Patentee of the Archimedian Screw Propeller", 31 December 1842, PRO, ADM/I S 22.

23 G. Penn, *Up Funnel, Down Screw* (London, 1955), 97.

24 A. Parry, *Parry of the Arctic* (London, 1963), 201.

25 *Illustrated London News*, 14 January 1843.

26 *The Artizan*, January 1843, Vol. 1, 28.

27 *London Journal of Commerce*, 14 October 1843.

28 *London Journal of Commerce*, 26 October 1843.

29 *Ibid* .

30 Port of London, Registration N 307 of 1843.

31 *London Journal of Commerce*, 14 October 1843.

32 Correspondence in PRO, ADM/1 5522.

33 *The Artizan*, October, 1843, Vol. 1, 246.

34 *Shipping & Mercantile Gazette*, London, 7 June 1845.

35 PRO, B 798/366, 708, 1101, 1315, 1669, 1959.

36 Anderson, *Sailing Ships*, 248.

37 Sholto Cooke, *The Maiden City and the Western Ocean* (Dublin, 1961), 56-7.

THE ROYAL NAVY AND THE INTRODUCTION OF THE SCREW PROPELLER, 1837-1847

Andrew Lambert

Introduction : The Royal Navy and Steam: Unthinking Opposition or Cautious Progress?

The conventional image of the Royal Navy and the development of the steamship remains that of Ericsson, Brunel and their apologists. They conclude that the Admiralty deliberately hampered pioneering efforts to adopt the steam engine, and each successive advance in steam technology, demonstrating that combination of blind prejudice and simple-minded ignorance commonly supposed to have marked all aspects of nineteenth-century military administration.[1] This paper will offer an alternative view, based on Admiralty files and private correspondence, to demonstrate the errors that earlier studies have fallen into from relying upon one-sided and inadequate sources.

The great nineteenth-century accounts, and those that adopt the same argument, reflect the technical historians' obsession with progress. This has encouraged the view that opposition to change, in engineering as in politics, is by definition wrong; ignoring the gulf in practical mechanics between first tests and effective exploitation. Caution should not be condemned in those called upon to meet a new development, based on novel, unproven technology, particularly with hindsight.

Nineteenth-century naval officers and their political masters had, in the main, very clear ideas of what they wanted to achieve with steam and understood the limitations of existing technology. Consequently their response to new developments was not unthinking animosity. Rather the policy makers of the nineteenth century, like those of any other period, were experienced men, conscious of their responsibility for the defence of an empire, based on the maintenance of naval supremacy. Their reluctance to tamper with the fabric of seapower was understandable, their willingness to take up new ideas, once the technology was proven, while commendable, was no more than their duty. In no single instance did the Royal Navy fall behind its major rivals in responding to practical manifestations of technological change. Perhaps the most rounded example of this policy came with HMS *Warrior* of 1861, still afloat in Portsmouth Harbour. Although only the second capital ship with armour, *Warrior* was the first with an internally subdivided iron hull, breech loading artillery, and the first to exploit the unlimited potential of iron shipbuilding. The individual elements were neither radical nor dangerous, proven technology was adopted and turned to serve British requirements.[2]

The Admiralty, the Surveyor's Department and the Steam Warship

Much adverse comment on the Admiralty's role in the adoption of the steam warship has appeared, but it should be stressed that the real problem was one of administrative structure, rather than decision making. In 1832 British naval administration was subjected to a comprehensive overhaul. The age-old distinction between the Admiralty – the Board charged with the execution of the duties of the Lord High Admiral, essentially the military direction of the navy – and the Navy and Victualling Boards, charged with the administration of the civil branch of the service, principally maintaining the fleet and feeding the men – ended. Daily superintendence of the administration of the navy was turned over to the Board of Admiralty, the Navy and Victualling Boards being abolished. Removing this level of administration saved a small amount of money, in accordance with the political programme of the whig party. However, the Navy Board had also been the source of sound advice on warship design and construction. In the following two decades, when the need for guidance was greater than ever before, there was no alternative source. In place of the Navy Board responsibility for ship design and construction was given to the Surveyor of the Navy, under the superintendence of the First Naval Lord. The Surveyor was a permanent official, unlike the Lords who would change with the government. Hitherto the Surveyor had always been a Dockyard-trained shipbuilder and a member of the Navy Board. As a part of the reform process the existing Surveyor was removed, his office being given to a naval officer, Captain William Symonds, noted for designing fast brigs. However the real import of the change was that the Surveyor must now be a policy maker, rather than a designer; he would have an assistant for detailed design work. Unfortunately Symonds was more interested in promoting his own design principles. Starved of funds to maintain the existing fleet and with no clear guidance from the First Naval Lord his department could do little to prepare long-term policies.[3] It was against this background, without a coherent long-term policy, that the Royal Navy had to respond to the screw propeller. In the confused vacuum of policy-making almost every member of the Admiralty Board had an opinion, and most were pressed on the First Lord.

To add to the confusion a new Department, that of Comptroller of Steam, had been created on 19 April 1837. The first incumbent, the Arctic explorer Captain Edward Parry, was no expert; his claims had more to do with the political influence of his brother-in-law, Lord Stanley of Alderley, patronage secretary of the Melbourne administration.[4] The expertise of the new department came from Peter Ewart, the conservative Boulton & Watt-trained chief engineer. The relationship between the Surveyor's Office and the Steam Department was only placed on a regular footing in February 1850, when the two departments were combined under the Surveyor, Captain Sir Baldwin Walker. Without clear instructions, Symonds, a far stronger character, all but ignored Parry. He believed the steam engine was an auxiliary element in any ship, so that the Steam Department had a duty to fit engines into his ships, rather than take part in a co-operative process. Symonds' broad-beamed hull form, with sharply rising floors, was ill suited to installing engines low in the hull, causing major problems for the Steam Department.

The Paddle Wheel Warship and Contemporary Tactics

Another error in many accounts of the introduction of steam into the world's navies concerns the role envisaged for the early steamers in fleet action. French theorists, searching for a 'Nouvelle Force Maritime' to overthrow British supremacy proposed using small steam gunboats to defeat sailing battlefleets. The poor seakeeping and gunnery performance of small vessels, and the primitive state of marine engineering in the first half of the nineteenth century made such proposals visionary. The alarm caused by such pamphlets in Britain reflected public ignorance, rather than official concern. From 1816 British policy makers were happy to consider the steamship as an auxiliary, primarily for towing. When urged to expedite the introduction of steam into the navy, Charles Wood, First Secretary at the Board, responded with a statement that was at once cautious and far-sighted:

> Your points about steamers and paddle wheels I am not competent to give an opinion upon, but I am strongly inclined to believe that neither the increased use of steam, nor that of shells and improved gunnery will diminish the advantages which this country has hitherto maintained at sea over other powers.[5]

Various misleading, often out of context, expressions have been quoted to establish that the war steamer was seen, from the very outset, as a major combat unit. This is quite inaccurate; steam warships were used as auxiliaries until the perfection of the screw line of battleship in 1851, and even then there were serious reservations about using steam in close action. The paddle steamer was never a front line warship, being used in subsidiary roles out of range of heavy sailing warships. During the Syrian campaign of 1840, culminating with the bombardment of Acre, 3 November 1840, British steamers fulfilled a variety of subordinate roles. At Acre it was intended they should tow the fleet into action. This plan was abandoned, the heavy ships going in under sail to make the close attack, the steamers engaging with shell guns at long range. At the bombardment of Sevastopol, 17 October 1854, British steamers towed the battlefleet into action lashed to the disengaged side of the heavy ships, the remainder engaged under way, at long range.

The armament of paddlewheel warships emphasised their difference from the sailing ship of similar size. With limited space on the broadside they mounted a reduced battery of heavy calibre guns, with pivot guns on the upper deck. Tactically limited by their weak armament and exposed machinery the paddle warship was condemned to an indecisive role at long range. The same heavy calibre upper deck battery was adopted for the early screw frigates *Dauntless* and *Arrogant*, and the first draught of the pioneer steam battleship *James Watt* in 1847, although the lower decks were armed as sailing ships. Unlike the paddle wheel ships the screw warship quickly adopted the normal broadside armament for line of battle tactics. In the early 1840s large paddle frigates were built as front rank warships, without success. The *Terrible* was larger than a 50-gun frigate, and very expensive, but she remained an overgrown tug and despatch boat. After 1847 new paddle steamers were limited to 1,000 tons, belated recognition of their auxiliary role.

The essential problem was one of vulnerability. Paddle steamers were only of value while they could use their engines, they were poor sailing ships, and did not have the armament to engage a heavy corvette. Therefore they had to avoid close action. While the paddle wheels were a large target, they were not vital and could withstand a great deal of damage. Behind them lay the more vulnerable crankshaft, connecting rods and boiler crowns. Further problems across from having so many sources of heat and fire in a warship. The Surveyor certainly saw this as the principal disqualification of the steamer, of whatever type, as a warship.[6] Equally problematic was the strategic relationship between the paddle frigate and the sailing battle fleet. Paddle wheel ships could not keep station under sail with the fleet, even if they unshipped their paddle boards. This reinforced the concept of the paddle frigate as an auxiliary warship. It had many uses, but its disadvantages ensured it remained a secondary element in naval power.

The Screw Propeller

As the paddle wheel warship, even in its most powerful form, remained an auxiliary the application of steam to the front line of naval warfare required a new form of propulsion. The screw propeller had one critical advantage, it could make steam an auxiliary in sailing warships. The concept of the auxiliary steamer was decisive for the Royal Navy.

The screw propeller was developed into a practical form by two men, working independently. The Swedish Army engineer John Ericsson was the first to attempt to interest the Royal Navy. His launch *Francis B. Ogden* towed the Admiralty barge from Somerset House to Seaward's engine works at Limehouse and back in the summer of 1837. Aboard were Admiral Sir Charles Adam, First Naval Lord, Symonds, Parry, Captain Francis Beaufort, the Hydrographer and others. According to Ericsson's biographer Beaufort's letter to the inventor, condemning his system as an utter failure, was largely influenced by Symonds. Symonds declared that while the screw was a propeller any method of propulsion working at the stern would ruin the steering; the Admiralty barge had been towed to disguise this fatal flaw.[7] Symonds' biographer made no mention of the incident, of Ericsson, of Pettit Smith or even the *Archimedes*. Ericsson's screw, a pair of contra-rotating bladed drums aft of the rudder, was over complex and, as the French discovered with the frigate *Pomone*, had a detrimental effect on steering.[8]   Certainly Ericsson's prospects improved when he removed one drum and placed his propeller ahead of the rudder.   His subsequent departure for the United States was not the end of his work in Europe, his countrymen Count Rosen and Holm secured trials of his later propeller in the tender *Bee*.   Later engines based on his design were built by Miller & Ravenhill and installed in the frigate *Amphion*.[9]   While some accounts contend that his propeller was also fitted it would appear that a more conventional type was used from the outset.[10]

The Englishman Francis Pettit Smith never claimed to have 'invented' the screw propeller, confining his patent of 31 May 1836 to the placing of the 'Archimedean' screw between the stern post and the rudder.   Smith's father had been tutor to Lord Sligo, and after trials of a boat using Smith's system Sligo helped fund the construction of the first seagoing screw vessel, aptly named *Archimedes*, in 1839, on the advice of Captain George Evans R.N.[11]   The Ship Propeller Company, formed to exploit the commercial opportunities of the screw propeller for naval and mercantile ships, built *Archimedes* as a mobile advertisement.

Archimedes, the Beginning of Naval and Mercantile Interest

Unlike the small open boats of Ericsson and Pettit Smith, *Archimedes* was a serious seagoing vessel, from which lessons could be taken directly to larger ships. Her dimensions were:

Length	125 feet extreme
	106' 8" between perpendiculars
Breadth	21' 10" extreme
Depth in hold	13'
Draught, Aft	10'
Forward	9'
Displacement	232 tons
Engines	80 nominal horse power by Rennie

This vessel, built at Blackwall by Henry Wimshurst, a member of the Company, was launched in November 1838.   She was demonstrated to the Admiralty on the Thames on 16 October 1839.   While no Lord of Admiralty attended, and the Company's request to tow a frigate was ignored, a party of naval officers, including Captains Parry, Symonds, George Evans, Francis Austin, William Shirreff and Basil Hall, the engineers Ewart, Miller, Charles Manby and Smith, and a number of the company's shareholders were aboard.[12]   *Archimedes* worked, but her underpowered machinery and bulky gearing were too large and noisy to be practical.   The propeller was geared for 127 rpm, 5 1/3 times engine speed.   Parry, used to the relative sophistication of Seaward's direct-acting paddle wheel engines, found the spur gearing bulky and noisy.   His report to the Secretary to the Admiralty, Charles Wood, emphasised the auxiliary nature of the invention.

Observing that her best speed was only 7 3/4 knots, far below the best paddle wheel vessels, he concluded: 'she is a nice little vessel, and a pretty model for sailing, which it seems to me they were anxious to combine with the screw experiment'.[13] This would be the key to success, rather than outright speed, where the paddlewheel vessel would have an advantage for another twenty years, from the limited knowledge of hull and propeller forms. George Evans, one of the first commissioned officers to command a steam vessel, also reported on the trial. His letter to Admiral Sir William Parker, the Second Naval Lord, ignored technical shortcomings, concentrating on the potential of the screw. He emphasised security from gunfire and the retention of the broadside, along with a standard rig, improved steering, and reduced strain on the engines from the constant immersion of the propeller. He concluded: 'the screw will supersede every other means hitherto adopted for propelling vessels'.[14] After this trial *Archimedes* was demonstrated to mercantile interests and sent on a round Britain promotional tour, which would have important results.

Sir William Symonds has commonly been blamed for the 'failure' of the Admiralty to adopt the screw propeller. The elevation of Brunel to the rank of the immortals has condemned him to play the part of the superstitious reactionary. This is inaccurate, and easily revised. Within days of the *Archimedes* trial Seawards submitted a plan to install screw engines of 60 nhp in 80-gun battleships. Symonds reported to the Board:

As this plan holds out many advantages for increasing the efficiency of a man of war, I am induced to submit the same for the consideration of their Lordships, and to observe that I see no difficulty to its being fitted in a ship of the *Vanguard*'s class, provided that the Magazine is not placed amidships and an alteration made in the position of the Funnel to clear the Launch on deck.[15]

Such an engine would provide manoeuvrability in a calm and the ability to leave harbour. Symonds, with almost every officer, considered steam a useful auxiliary. He was quite happy to install it in his beloved sailing ships, to add to their qualities. His opposition to the screw was as a principal means of propulsion, when the requirements of steam affected the design of ships to the detriment of the sailing qualities he had devoted his professional life to developing. On this occasion the Board, despite Symonds' advice, declined Seaward's plan.[16]

Archimedes' impact on the Navy was increased by a series of cross-channel races she ran with the Dover Packets from May 1840. After modifications she proved a match for the regular paddle wheel vessels, once her relative size and power had been taken into account. Having established the validity of the concept, both as an auxiliary and for full power, it only remained to decide how the new, and still largely experimental, development should be introduced into the navy. There were several possibilities, the line proposed by Seawards and supported by Symonds, further experiment with small vessels, or the construction or conversion of a larger ship. Given the level of technology further experiment was vital to exploit the potential of the screw. The decisions taken by the Admiralty must be viewed against this background.

Brunel, *The Great Britain,* **and the Admiralty**

As part of her promotional tour *Archimedes* called at Bristol in May 1840, creating an immediate impression on the Building Committee of the Great Western Steamship Company. Construction of the iron steamship was halted, to consider the new system. After initial reluctance to believe in the system, Brunel, the leading engineer, supported the decision and was deputed to investigate the screw propeller. He chartered *Archimedes* in the summer, conducting a series of comparative trials with different designs of propeller and compared the motion of the new vessel with the *Great Western,* before producing his report of 10 October 1840. This carefully argued paper set out the engineering and mechanical advantages, and although some of the data was unreliable his conclusions were firmly in favour of the screw. He noted the compromise hull form of the trials' vessel, but did not draw the same conclusion as Parry, because he was only interested in the screw as a prime mover, not an auxiliary. This basic point of departure between the Admiralty policymakers and the engineer has never been given due weight in explaining their differences. Brunel shared Ewart's critical opinion of the gearing, and considered the original screw inefficient.[17] The ship under construction was *The Great Britain,* the largest merchant ship of the decade and the pioneer of many important developments. While she was of great interest to the Royal Navy she remained, for the navy, more significant as a theoretical demonstration than a serious model. *The Great Britain* was a full-powered screw steamship with auxiliary sail, designed for a specific role. The navy would not build a large full-powered screw steamship for almost two decades.

The importance of *The Great Britain* lay in the prestige she conferred on Brunel. An ardent convert to the screw, Brunel provided the Admiralty with a copy of his report and, as the engineering consultant for the navy's pioneer screw steam warship, ensured the service kept up with the experience that shaped his own project. Uniquely Brunel had the vision and the courage to adopt the screw at once. No more large full-powered screw steamships were built in the 1840s, the reasons for this were primarily technological, although financial risk played a part. The mercantile shipping community was, if anything, more cautious than the navy. This was not surprising when many of them were dealing directly with their own money, and had only recently become adjusted to the impact of the paddle wheel; later the fate of the *Great Northern* must have been known throughout the shipping community. Brunel was neither a shipowner nor a naval architect, he relied on engineering principles. Seeing his great project in hand, and well aware of his success with the *Great Western* it was natural Parry should recommend that Brunel advise the Admiralty on the new system.[18] Brunel had the singular advantage of having no financial stake in the success of the screw, unlike Smith, who had already been approached.

Naval interest in the screw depended upon the practical application of the system, not a demonstration of theoretical potential. Captain Chappell, liaising with the Propeller Company, proposed building a replica of any existing paddle wheel vessel to try the screw, and fitting a frigate for experiments on a larger scale. The first concept looked toward a full-powered screw steamer, the second contained the germ of the *Great Northern*. The first ship proposed for conversion was the half-built paddle sloop *Shearwater*. While Ewart considered her engines could be converted to drive a screw, Parry proposed building a new vessel.[19] The Ship Propeller Company objected to the ship, and Symonds supported all their arguments, raising no objection to the screw during 1840. The First Lord, Lord Minto, concurred.[20] After their experience aboard *Archimedes* Parry and Ewart considered the problems of geared drive. Ewart, like Brunel, concluded there was no need for the noise and inconvenience of the original arrangement. In consequence Parry advised the construction of an experimental vessel, a replica of the 200 nhp Mediterranean-packet *Polyphemus*. The new ship would use identical engines, with her stern configured to allow modification and testing alternative screws.[21] More immediately the Board sanctioned the modification of the 42-ton tender *Bee*, an instructional steam vessel for the Gunnery Training Ship HMS *Excellent*, to carry a screw <u>and</u> paddles.[22] Pettit Smith and Captain Chappell were consulted on this curious project. Minto's Admiralty Board was enthusiastic for the screw propeller, prepared to sanction expenditure and sensible of the pioneering work conducted outside the Steam and Surveyor's Departments. It would be absurd to suggest that this Board opposed the introduction of the screw propeller.

Having decided to build a sister to *Polyphemus*, a model of her stern was sent to the Ship Propeller Company (No. 15 Fish Street Hill), for the attention of Smith and Chappell. Symonds was far from pleased by the reply, which required an opening 8 feet long and 9 feet 3 inches deep, this, he noted, 'tends to weaken the ship ... particularly if she strikes the ground'.[23] This early dispute between the Surveyor and the Steam Department must have had a bearing on Parry's decision to involve Brunel, who was invited to oversee the project after an interview with Minto on 27 April 1841. The role of Christopher Claxton, a Royal Navy lieutenant on half pay as well as a leading member of the Great Western Steamship Company, has never been established, although it appears certain that, from his earlier correspondence with Parry, he was instrumental in bringing his friend's merits to the notice of the Steam Department.[24] Brunel sent in drawings covering the application of the screw to a vessel of *Polyphemus* class, and was requested to await further communications from the Board. Brunel requested a clear statement of his role in the project, and Parry was quick to reply.[25]

My Dear Sir,

I have just received your letter of 28th from St. Ives, and I hasten to say that it was entirely understood by myself, as Lord Minto's wish, that you should have the sole responsibility and consequently the sole direction of the mechanical arrangements for making trial of the Screw Propeller in a vessel to be built as a Sister Ship to the *Polyphemus*, and so far as I am aware this understanding is still in full force. Not having the papers by me at this moment, I cannot refer to the exact course which I submitted to the Board of Admiralty, upon the receipt of your report, but I am quite sure that there neither was, nor is, the smallest intention of allowing any <u>interference</u> with your own views on the part of the Admiralty Engineers,and you; and you may depend upon it that there will be none.

All that our Engineer Officers will have to do is to assist in carrying forward your views and I do not recollect that their report or opinion has been called for, except in the question which <u>you</u> referred for a decision to the Admiralty. I mean the question as to what manufacturer should be called upon to make the Engines. The result has been that two of the three named by you have been invited to tender, and thus I think the matter rests. No tender will be accepted without reference to you. At least if my views are followed, and I do not see how, under these circumstances you need apprehend any interference whatever.

At all events I wish to venture to say that, if anything occurs approaching to such interference, I hope you will mention it to me, and I will do everything in my power to set the matter right, and in so doing I am sure that I shall be acting in the full spirit of their Lordships' intentions in this matter. I may add that I know it to be Mr. Ewart's special wish that you should have the entire arrangment of the whole, and I am confident that he will be ready and willing to assist in carrying out your views.

W.E. Parry

I.K. Brunel

The interference to which Parry referred was, by inference, expected from Symonds, rather than Ewart, who was quite prepared to turn over the screw project to Brunel. After visiting *Polyphemus* with Symonds, Brunel recommended that Maudslay, Son & Field provide a 200-nhp engine of the 'Siamese' design.[26] At this stage Smith, who was also involved, requested some elucidation of his position, and that of Brunel. Accordingly Minto, Adam, Symonds, Parry, Chappel, Brunel, Smith and Ewart assembled in Minto's room in late September. In view of the work

Brunel had already carried out both for the Great Western Company and the Admiralty, Parry recommended that he be admitted to the 'conference' on the screw propeller.[27] Symonds agreed, but observed that the opening specified by Brunel was larger and required more draught than that of Smith. Both features were, in his mind, serious objections.[28]

At this stage the relationship between Brunel and the Admiralty was thrown into confusion by a change of administration, Lord Melbourne's whig government being replaced by Sir Robert Peel's conservative ministry during September. The change broke up a team committed to large-scale experiments, and removed from office Lord Minto, who had supported Parry in calling on Brunel for advice. The leading men of Peel's Admiralty were the First Naval Lord, Admiral Sir George Cockburn, and the political Secretary, Sidney Herbert. The First Lord, Lord Haddington, deferred to them in their respective areas of expertise. While the new team settled into their work the role of Brunel was thrown into question, his understanding with Parry being unofficial. Brunel was not without supporters in positions of influence. Within days of the new Board taking office the Commander-in-Chief at Portsmouth, Admiral Sir Edward Codrington, urged Herbert to consider placing steam engines on the orlop deck of battleships and frigates, to prevent paddle steamers taking up positions to rake them when becalmed.[29] Codrington, a leading radical on the left of the whig party, had been a supporter of the Thames Tunnel and his connections with the Brunels were of long standing.[30] It is probable Codrington's letter was prompted, for he continued to urge Brunel's plans.[31] With the change of administration Brunel, who shared the radical sympathies of his brother-in-law, Benjamin Hawes, lost many friends in high places. Only Parry remained, and he had little influence with the new Board. It is possible that Brunel's politics had a bearing on the attitude of the Admiralty toward him, and the Great Western Steamship Company.

On the first day of 1842 Brunel was recalled to the Admiralty for discussions with Parry and Symonds.[32] The new Board favoured a return to cheap screw experiments, using an existing vessel to carry the engines already ordered. Following the meeting on the 6th Symonds requested that Maudslays provide details of the 200 nhp engines, in particular the space they would require, to determine if they would fit the 180 nhp steamer *Acheron*. While the Admiralty concurred, Symonds noted that the new engine would be 40 nhp more powerful than the existing paddle wheel engine by Seaward, making the trial results unreliable. The vessel would be elongated by four feet at the stern to incorporate an aperture 9' 6" deep and 5' long. Parry queried whether Brunel and Maudslays should be informed; Symonds considered that a bare statement of intent to place the engines in *Acheron* would be adequate.[33] Within days Symonds was authorised to give directions to the Captain Superintendent at Woolwich, the base and building yard of the steam navy.[34] Brunel requested details of *Acheron*, returning a strong critique of the ship as a trials vehicle.[35]

18 Duke Street, Westminster
Feby, 10, 1842

70

Sir,

I have received from Sir Wm. Symonds the drawings of the Acheron with a sketch of the alterations which the stern admits of, for the purpose of applying a Screw and all other information respecting the Vessel which I have required.

I have to request that you will represent to the Lord Commissioners of the Admiralty that I am convinced that the attempt to apply a Screw propeller to this Vessel will not answer any of the objects which their Lordships have in view.

Firstly – The Screw Propeller as I have stated in my former communications and as will be evident to their Lordships when they consider the position in which it is placed, requires that the Vessel should have a very fine run. The Acheron is on the contrary very full abaft – much more so than even the Polyphemus which although a very excellent model for paddles would still require some modification for the Screw.

I have subjoined half breadth plans of the Acheron and the Polyphemus and of the Archimedes in which the Screw has been successfully applied, by which the very great difference in their forms will be seen.

Secondly – The Acheron is built with Sponsons which cannot therefore be removed and when the paddle boxes are taken away, at the best, the spaces can only be filled up – but even in this state the Vessel cannot, I apprehend, be considered a good sailing ship.

I have no hesitation in saying the Vessel so altered will be comparatively an inefficient steam-boat, inferior to what she would be if left as a paddle-boat – while as an experiment with the Screw no result can be obtained because she is not at all adapted for the Screw and because the Engines to be used being much more powerful than those which have hitherto worked her no conclusion can consequently be drawn from the comparisons of the speed attained.

In conclusion I must beg strongly to urge upon their Lordships if they are still desirous of determining whether the Screw is equal or superior to the paddles for all or any of the objects required in Government Steam-ships, that this point can be determined only by building and rigging a vessel expressly adapted to the Screw, and as nearly as possible of the same dimensions and with the same power as some of the best paddle Steam-boats with which her different qualities under different circumstances can be tested – that this mode of making the experiment will be the only effectual one and will eventually cause much the least waste of time and as a very good Steam-boat will at all events be obtained, it cannot be considered as involving any waste of money or any expense for the mere experiment.

I have the honour to be
Sir
Your obedient Servant

71

Sir John Barrow, Bart
Secretary to the Admiralty

endorsed
Feby 18 send this to Sir W. Symonds and desire him to report any
Steamer now in progress of building he considers fit to receive the
engines ordered for the Screw, and he thinks could be adapted or
altered for that purpose and to communicate with
Sir E. Parry and Mr. Brunel.
Sidney Herbert

(PRO, ADM 83/25, S2407)

While Herbert's endorsement demonstrated that at least one man at the
Admiralty was prepared to take up his predecessor's work there was another side to
the problem, and one which Brunel had not considered. The Admiralty were
interested in the screw as an auxiliary in vessels still primarily reliant upon sail.
Further, any hull form they adopted had to support concentrated weights of heavy
artillery at all points, including the bow and stern. Therefore the ideal fine stern run
could not be achieved in a wooden warship without compromising the structural
integrity of the vessel. As late as 1850 the ambition of the Admiralty in adopting
screw propulsion for large warships was limited to a speed of 6 knots.[36] The
hydrodynamic requirements for such limited performance were very different from
those of a full-powered steamer. In proposing the *Acheron* as a trials vessel the
Admiralty was not trying to spoil the experiment, rather they were demonstrating
that their interest lay in the auxiliary use of the screw. At this juncture Brunel was
the only proponent of the screw for use in full-powered steamers. The Ship
Propeller Company was more interested in auxiliary use, as the *Archimedes*
demonstrated. Smith, unlike Brunel, was looking to the universal adoption of his
system, and this could not be accomplished with full-powered ships, given the
technology of the period.

Following Herbert's endorsement an official minute was sent the next day.
Symonds observed that the steamers then building were too large for the 200 nhp
engines and recommended a return to the plan of December 1840, constructing a
replica of *Polyphemus* at Sheerness in place of the paddle sloop *Rattler* which had
been suspended some time previously. This was approved on February 24, the
sheer draught being submitted on 6 April.[37] The drawings were approved, Symonds
being directed to transmit copies to, and proceed 'in communication with Mr.
Smith'.[38] The remaining drawings, scantlings and profiles were sent to Sheerness
as soon as they could be prepared, the profile, for example, being sent on 1 July.[39]
This reflected urgency, not delay. It should be stressed that *Rattler* was a new
design, using seasoned timber prepared for a larger 280-nhp paddle wheel sloop of
the *Styx* class. She was not converted from any existing ship. The selection of

Rattler only reflected the importance of seasoned timber in the post-1815 navy. This, and not an attempt to hide the ship, as Brunel's panegyrists argue, was the reason she was built at Sheerness, the least of all the navy's building yards, inconveniently situated at the mouth of the Medway, miles from the heart of the steam navy.[40]

Dimensions

Length	176.6 feet between perpendiculars – 164.0 as a paddle wheel vessel
Breadth	32.8 feet extreme
Breadth, for tonnage	32.6 feet
Depth in Hold	18.7 feet
Draught,Mean	12.11 inches
Burthen, in Tons	866 80/94
Displacement	1112 tons
Engines	200 nominal horse power Vertical 'Siamese' driving through straps, by Maudslay, Son & Field
	4 cylinders 25 rpm approximately 300 indicated horse power
Propeller	Smith type

Brunel was not immediately informed, because he was in Italy. On his return he learned that the work was in hand, with Smith advising the Shipwright Officers.[41] Smith provided details of the screw aperture, the screw and the gearing required.[42]

15 Fish St. Hill
June 4th, 1842

Sir Wm. Symonds
Surveyor of the Navy

Sir,
Having been instructed to prepare a drawing of the actual dimensions required for the application of the Screw Propeller to H M   Ship Rattler, I beg to forward the accompanying sketch which describes the whole in section, and should any further particulars be required I shall hold myself in readiness to attend at Somerset House or elsewhere.
I am Sir,
Your obedient Servant
F.P. Smith

Proportions of the Screw Machinery for H M Steamer Rattler

	Feet	Inches
Diameter of Screw	9	
Pitch	11	
Area of Screw	63	6
Opening of Deadwood in the Clear	9	6 high
" " " " " " " " "	8	0 long
Revolutions required per minute	112	
Diameter of Cog Wheel	15	
" " Pin	3	4
3 series of Cogs of 6 inches each 6 inches Pitch		
Breadth of Cogs in the face		22
Multiple 4 1/2 to one of the Engine		
Engine to make 25 strokes per minute		
Height of Crankshaft from base plate	13	
Distance of Crankshaft from underside of Keel	15	3
Distance between Crankshaft and propeller Shaft	9	3
Centre of screw Shaft from the underside of Keel	6	3
Depth of Keel and metal Knee below the Screw	1	6
With metal plates on each side the entire depth of Keep and united through all		

(PRO, ADM 87/12,S3361)

Realising he was being ignored Brunel complained to Herbert. The Admiralty order of 6 April had not mentioned Brunel, leading Symonds to surmise he had no further role in the process. In response Herbert restated the original intention of the Minto Board, that Brunel should oversee the installation of the screw in communication with Smith and Symonds.[43] Brunel was to liaise with Maudslays and the Captain Superintendent to ensure the successful installation of the machinery.[44]

Far from wanting to delay the ship Symonds was annoyed to find, on a visit to Sheerness, that her after body was suspended, 'on account of the indecision of the Engineers who are to provide a screw propeller for her'. He urged that Smith and

Brunel act immediately.[45] Brunel was already conferring with Maudslays and, on visiting Sheerness found the deadwood almost complete, according to Smith's plan, to which he recommended only slight modification. He stressed the need for the iron work of the stern to be prepared by Maudslays, as it would have to fit accurately with the screw shaft. In contrast to the apoplectic First Naval Lord portrayed by Brunel, Cockburn endorsed his letter, sending it to Symonds for his 'information and guidance'.[46] Later Brunel claimed the delay had been caused by illness.[47]

Another visit to Sheerness, in company with Joshua Field from Maudslay, Son & Field, led Brunel to alter the position of the engines, shifting some deck beams without affecting the masts. These alterations were of little consequence, the ship being only half complete. Maudslays submitted the final engine and propeller drawings at the same time.[48]

Launched in April 1843 *Rattler* received her engines in the East India Docks, carrying out her first proving run on 30 October and made over 8 knots the following week with Brunel and Smith aboard. She then ran down the Thames with her half sister *Polyphemus*, proving the faster of the two. Contrary to received opinion the failure to copper the ship before this run was normal procedure. At that period steam machinery was installed by the engine builders in commercial basins. The ship could only be coppered, in a royal dockyard, after the engines had been installed. *Rattler*'s first trial was carried immediately after the installation of her machinery, before she was docked at Woolwich for her copper. Far from showing the Surveyor's animosity to the ship, the early trial before coppering demonstrated the Admiralty's enthusiasm for the screw, and a desire to test it at the first opportunity.[49]

In June 1843 the Admiralty purchased the small iron screw steamer *Mermaid*, renamed *Dwarf*, as a trials vessel to complement *Rattler*. She had been built by Ditchburn & Mare for trials with Rennie's conoidal propeller. Rennie's sold her for £5,350.

Dimensions

Length	130 feet extreme
Breadth	16 feet extreme
Draught, Aft	7 feet
Forward	5' 10"
Displacement	164 tons
Engines	90 nominal horse power direct acting by Rennie
	40" bore 2' 8" stroke 30 rpm light, 28 sea trim
Boilers	2 iron 6lb pressure 14 tons of water
Screw	2 blade Smith design 4' 5" 159 rpm, originally three-bladed Rennie conoidal

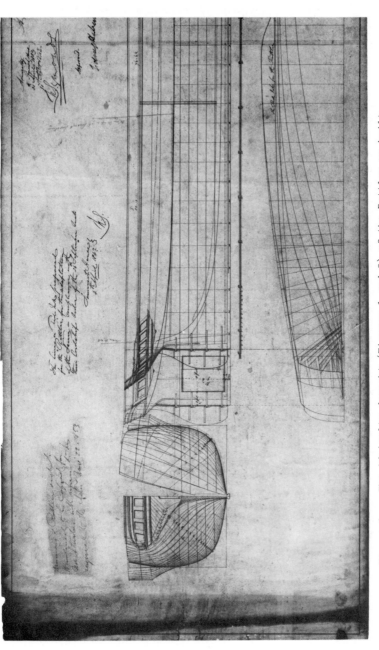

Figure 1. The Admiralty draught (Figures 1 and 2) of the Rattler as built.
Dated 6 April 1842. The draught was prepared from, and superimposed over
that of the Prometheus, a sister ship of the Polyphemus. The later design
is inked in red on the original, although the points of departure are clear
enough on this monotone reproduction. The elongation of the (cont. on Fig. 2)

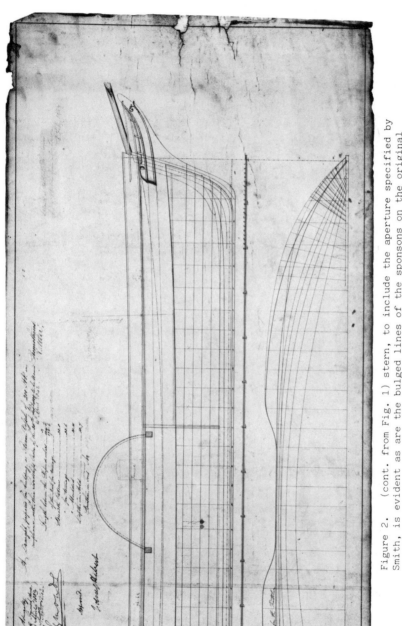

Figure 2. (cont. from Fig. 1) stern, to include the aperture specified by Smith, is evident as are the bulged lines of the sponsons on the original paddle wheel design. The principal modification lay in the addition of 12 feet 6 inches to the length between perpendiculars. The draught was signed by Symonds, and approved by Herbert. (National Maritime Museum)

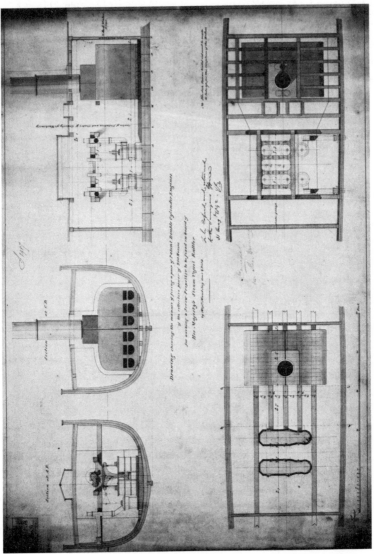

Figure 3. The engine drawings of the *Rattler*, showing the high level crankshaft, a legacy of the paddle wheel origins of the engines. This, with the attendant gearing and the crowns of the boilers, was exposed to gunfire above the waterline, a fundamental weakness that later engine designs would overcome. (National Maritime Museum)

Dwarf proved ideal; her size ensured she was easily docked and could run in the river, a useful quality for a ship based at Woolwich. As a purpose-built screw steamer *Dwarf* had a well contrived stern run. In service from early 1843, her stern was subjected to numerous modifications, testing many different propellers. During her ten-year career she was docked on nine occasions, three for the stern-run experiments, the remainder for repairs, painting and varnish. Modifications to the ship, with running repairs and coal, cost £5,600. Much of the resulting data was used to select modifications for *Rattler*, and to design later screw warships. She was sold in 1853 for £500, having made a major contribution to the development of the screw steam navy.

By contrast *Great Northern*, built on speculation as an experimental ship, was, as demonstrated in the preceding paper, an over-ambitious failure. Her builder would appear to have been influenced by a rumour current in late 1841 that the Admiralty would build or purchase a screw steamer for trials. John Laird of Birkenhead, a leading iron shipbuilder, proposed modifying a half built 800-ton iron paddle steamer, and took the opportunity to state the advantages of iron, giving strength to the screw aperture and installing watertight compartments.[50] A senior foreman from Woolwich inspected the vessel, but while Symonds acknowledged iron ships were strong and suitable for the screw, he concluded the existing vessel was too small and shallow aft.[51] The interest of the navy in *Great Northern*, offered for sale or hire as a transport, was serious. The Admiralty ordered a report on her fitness for service as a troopship. Symonds selected William Blessley, a leading dockyard foreman from Woolwich, to inspect the ship at Londonderry. Blessley's report was sufficient to damn the hull of the ship, while first sight of her engines damned the whole project. The opinions of Parry and Thomas Lloyd, who had replaced Ewart as Chief Engineer (Ewart was killed by a swinging chain hoist in Woolwich yard during 1842) on the engines are not available, but it is unlikely they would differ from those of *The Artizan*. With a purpose-built trials vessel in hand, built to naval standards with the best advice and machinery, there was no reason to take on a far larger vessel of doubtful quality. Later attempts to interest the Admiralty in the ship had at least as much to do with the Ship Propeller Company, who submitted copies of her log, as her owners. *Great Northern* never went to sea as a commercial merchant ship, either under steam or sail thus demonstrating the risks inherent in outstripping technology. The original engines of *The Great Britain* were based on a tried design of Brunel's father. The early 1840s were not the time to be working on the design of new machinery for full-powered or large auxiliary screw steamships. Within a decade John Penn's trunk engine and Maudslay's return connecting rod designs provided excellent performance and reliability. Admiralty interest in *Great Northern* was renewed in February 1846, while preparing a list of all large merchant steamers capable of carrying guns; but there was no reason to purchase the Londonderry albatross.[52]

Technological Progress, Strategic Problems and the Practical Steam Warship

Rattler, for all her success as a steam screw auxiliary, was far from perfect as a warship. Her machinery was exposed to the same degree as her paddle-wheel half sisters. The 'Siamese' engine was configured for a high-level paddle shaft, in *Rattler* the drive to the gearing was taken off just below the upper deck, well above the waterline. The Propeller Company, aware of the space wasted by the indirect drive, proposed a geared crankshaft in mid-1844 that would remove the need for the indirect gearing, used in all previous screw steamships, saving space and confining all machinery 'within a few feet of the Kelson of any vessel'. The first ship the Admiralty proposed to fit with the new system was the converted frigate *Amphion* (which was eventually fitted with direct acting engines based on Ericsson's designs), the first to enter service the sloop *Niger*.[53] In many ways this was the crucial achievement for the screw, allowing it to fill the role of auxiliary power in sailing ships, as the projectors had hoped. *Rattler* remained an experimental vessel, being used as such for the remainder of the 1840s. Even before her famous cruise with Admiral Sir William Parker's squadron in 1846, she had proved the validity of the screw auxiliary, which was far more important than races and a tug-of-war with her half sister *Alecto*. In 1844 and 1845 the Admiralty ordered the construction and conversion of several large screw steamers, from modified two deckers to iron frigates. Cockburn, the most influential naval policymaker between 1841 and 1846 was convinced, and took the opportunity to mock Sir Charles Napier for selecting the paddle wheel when allowed to build a war steamer of his own design:

> The proof we have lately had of the efficiency of the screw as a propeller on board of the *Rattler* convinced me, that it will be in future generally adopted & we are now adapting those building for that description of propeller.[54]

There was a degree of urgency in the decision. Concern over relations with France led Peel's administration to sanction a large expenditure on steamships, several of which were screw vessels. Reflecting the ambition of the Board, and the level of expertise available, these were auxiliary vessels with stern lines very different from those urged by Brunel. Believing Symonds' steamers were all failures Cockburn called for alternative designs from the Surveyor's most bitter critics.[55] Aware of the want of trust in the highest quarters Symonds conducted a bitter rearguard action, alienating friend and foe alike. In large part this was based on political quarrels dating back to 1832. Symonds, although a permanent official, continued to support his whig friends out of office.[56] Such internal warfare did nothing to ease the development of the screw, or encourage objective analysis.

In the 1840s experiments were more important than construction, where the French, and other navies, lagged far behind. Further, not one of the ships built before 1850 was entirely successful, from a combination of poor machinery and limited hydrodynamic knowledge. *Rattler* and *Dwarf* provided the empirical data to build an auxiliary steam navy. Symonds was well aware of the new thinking on hull forms for the screw.[57] He objected to the effect the new form would have on sailing qualities, because he could not bring himself to treat steamers as front line warships, or rely on engines. Men in more powerful positions had different ideas. Writing in 1848, Lord Auckland, then First Lord in Russell's whig administration, stressed that the steam auxiliary was the warship of the future. Early trials with the three-masted screw schooner *Reynard*, demonstrated the benefit of experience with *Rattler* and *Dwarf*. Launched at Deptford on 21 March 1848, the 516-ton *Reynard* (148' x 27.5") carried 8 32-pounders. In the Brig trials of that year, she proved almost equal to the purpose-built sailing craft, without having to resort to steam. Many sceptics were convinced, among them the Admiral in charge of the trials, Sir Charles Napier.[58] Realising Napier still favoured powerful paddle frigates, Auckland declared:

> I am satisfied that the whole theory of ship building will be directed from
> the old notions of sailing ships to the manner in which the screw
> auxiliary may be best combined with good sailing qualities.[59]

This meant abandoning Symonds controversial, wide-beamed hull for a stretched version of the older form. Adding length to sailing hulls sacrificed manoeuvrability and speed to windward for effective use of the screw; as a bonus the new hulls also provided improved sailing performance off the wind in favourable conditions, leaving steam to solve the problems of windward sailing that had long exercised the genius of shipbuilders and architects. This solution, of classic simplicity, made the steam auxiliary a far more effective warship than any that had gone before.

Other developments were vital to the success of the steam warship. The tubular boiler, first used by the Royal Navy aboard the paddle frigate *Penelope* of 1843, reduced the weight and space of the steam generating plant, allowing smaller machinery spaces, or more powerful engines. With the geared crankshaft and improved, direct acting engines configured for the screw propeller the boilers, perfected in the 1840s, were widely used in the following decade. The gap in reliability and performance between 1840 and 1850 was fundamental.

The rate at which the Royal Navy took up steam power, and later made it the principal method of propulsion, was determined by the progress of technology in relation to British strategic requirements. France built the full-powered steam battleship *Napoleon* in 1851 to escort military convoys between Toulon and Algiers, reflecting limited strategic requirements. The Royal Navy had converted four small steam battleships in the 1840s for local defence, but, like all British wooden steam battleships, these were auxiliary steamships. The superior performance of British engines tended to obscure the point, but British ships were designed for world-wide operations, with cruising under sail a priority. Steam remained an auxiliary, tactical, power until the 1860s.[60]

The full-powered steam warship, like the screw propeller, was adopted by the Royal Navy when it became practical; indeed the world's first ocean-going ship without sails was the British twin-screw turret battleship *Devastation*, of 1873. The move to mastless warships has been attributed to the impact of the *Captain* disaster of 1870 and improved steaming economy.

One factor yet to receive due weight is manpower. The crew of a sailing warship was based on the number and calibre of its guns; early steamships were given an engine room complement in addition. With crews for 50 to 130 guns large warships had the manpower to use a heavy square rig. For *The Great Britain*, operating in totally different conditions, Brunel designed a novel auxiliary rig to complement the engines on the North Atlantic passage, this had the added benefit of requiring a very small deck crew.[61] *Warrior* was rigged as an 80-gun ship of the line, with which she shared a crew of 750 men. This rig was now the back-up for a simple, single screw machinery plant. It was rendered unnecessary by the compound engine, watertube boilers and the twin screw installation. Randolph & Elder's compound engine was tried in the 50-gun frigate *Constance* in 1861, but proved over complex. The system was adopted in the early 1870s, after further trials in corvettes; the *Alexandra* of 1877 being the first battleship with compound engines.[62] The triple expansion engine of the 1880s marked the final triumph of steam over sail for all eventualities.

Conclusions

British policymakers were anxious to exploit the screw propeller, to maintain or improve the ability of the Royal Navy to control the sea. This reflected the strategic position of Britain, an island state with a worldwide empire based on seapower. While they could not afford to ignore any development in their field, they were not interested in progress for its own sake, only in practical, proven systems. While private industry was prepared to make the running, and bear the cost of pioneering efforts such as *Archimedes*, there was no good reason for the Admiralty to duplicate their efforts. The navy did have a role in the development of the screw propeller, to perfect it as a suitable auxiliary for warships. The historiographical myth that the Admiralty were behindhand, or positively hostile toward the screw, is long overdue for revision. Steam was adopted and given an increasing role in naval affairs as technological progress allowed mechanical engineering to match the expectations of the pioneers.

The legend of obstructionism reflects the administrative problems of a weakened and politically divided Admiralty. This caused unnecessary confusion, most apparent in relations between Brunel, Smith, Parry and Symonds, all of whom favoured the screw, within their own limits. The myth that the Admiralty, or more particularly Symonds, hampered Brunel should be dismissed. Brunel's real complaint was that the tory Admiralty did not maintain a personal agreement made with the whig Board. At a personal level he was not alone in finding Symonds difficult; Parry was simply brushed aside, leaving his role to Herbert. Herbert, the leading progressive at the Admiralty between 1841 and 1845 influenced Cockburn. When he moved to the War Office this role, and many of his papers, were passed to his successor, Henry Corry.[63] The removal of Symonds, and the redefinition of the Surveyor's duties, ensured that the creation of a steam navy was carried through smoothly. Symonds was not, however, as generally presumed, dismissed because of his opposition to the screw. The problems were administrative and personal. The post of Surveyor required a thorough overhaul, and as Symonds was difficult to work with, and of age for superannuation, he was manoeuvred into retirement by Lord Auckland, the First Lord, before the department was reformed. Even so Auckland requested his opinions on steamships a year later.[64] The new Surveyor, Captain Sir Baldwin Walker, was appointed as a policy maker, not a designer. He created the steam navy of the 1850s without the controversy and bitterness that surrounded his predecessor.

NOTES

1 G.S. Graham's widely followed paper 'The Transition from Paddle Wheel to Screw Propeller', *Mariner's Mirror*, 44 (1958), 35-48, adopts this critical approach to naval policymakers, lauding private individuals. However, the basic theme of naval opposition to the steam engine was refuted in P.W. Brock and Basil Greenhill, *Sail and Steam* (Newton Abbot, 1973),11, 12. Further work on the origins of the steam navy will, as this paper suggests in the instance of the screw propeller, provide a more accurate, and more favourable appreciation of naval decision making in the period 1815-1850.

2 A.D. Lambert, *Warrior, the World's First Ironclad* (London, 1987).

3 A.D. Lambert, 'Captain Sir William Symonds and the Ship of the Line; 1832-1847', *Mariner's Mirror*, Vol. 74 (1987), 167-79. J.A. Sharp, *Memoirs of the Life and Services of Rear Admiral Sir William Symonds* (London, 1858). A one-sided eulogy of Symonds, composed under the terms of his will, and mainly concerned with his sailing ships.

4 A. Parry, *Parry of the Arctic* (London, 1963).

5 H-J. Paixhans, *Nouvelle Force Maritime* (Paris, 1821); Sir J. Barrow, *An Autobiographical Memoir* (London,1847), 388; Charles Wood to Captain Charles Napier, 17 December 1838, National Maritime Museum, (hereafter NMM) Napier MSS, Nap. 20.

6   Symonds to Lord Auckland, 23 November 1848, NMM, WWL/1, Papers of
    Admiral Sir Baldwin Walker.

7   W.C. Church, *The Life of John Ericsson* (London, 1891), Vol. 1, 89. The first
    screw propelled vessel to be given a successful trial would appear to have been
    the *Little Juliana* of 1804, built by the American inventor John Stevens and
    tried at Hoboken in May 1804. Although he continued experiments for another
    decade and obtained a British patent, Stevens later transferred his attention to
    paddle wheel vessels. H.P. Spratt, *The Birth of the Steam Boat* (London, 1958),
    70-2.

8   H.M. Consul at Cherbourg to the Admiralty, 9 January 1847, Public Record
    Office (hereafter not cited), ADM 87/17. The consuls in French dockyard
    towns received double pay in return for a regular supply of information.

9   Admiralty to Surveyor, 6 November 1843, ADM 83/30, S7866; ordering the
    trial of the propeller under the superintendence of Mr Holm. Using *Bee* for the
    trial indicated the anxiety of the Admiralty to try the system, they having no
    other vessel available fitted for screw propulsion.

10 Admiralty to Surveyor, 18 June 1844, ADM 83/32, S1416, accepting Rosen
    and Miller & Ravenhill's tender for the engines of *Amphion*. E.C. Smith, *A
    Short History of Marine Engineering* (Cambridge, 1938), 68, and Admiral Sir
    P. Colomb, *Memoirs of Sir Astley Cooper Key* (London, 1898), 221, both
    contend that an Ericsson screw was fitted, but the as-fitted draught published in
    A.D. Lambert, *Battleships in Transition. The Creation of the Steam Battlefleet,
    1815-1860* (London, 1983), at pp.22-3, indicates that the propeller was in fact
    of the Smith type, although not a particularly efficient form.

11 *A Record of the Services of Admiral George Evans* (London, 1876), 30.

12 C.A. Caldwell to Henry Tufnell, 4 October 1839, NMM, Minto Papers,
    ELL/233.

13 Parry to Sir Charles Wood, 18 October 1839, in *Parry of the Arctic*, 203-4.

14 Evans to Parker, 23 October 1839, in *Record of Admiral Evans*, 11-13.

15 Surveyor to Admiralty, 30 October 1839, ADM 92/9, p. 52.

16 Surveyor to Seaward Brothers, 9 October 1839, ADM 91/9, S191.

17 E. Corlett, *The Iron Ship* (Bradford on Avon, 1975), 54-61; I.K. Brunel, *Life of
    Isambard Kingdom* Brunel (London, 1870), 539-58.

18 Parry to Claxton, 12 July 1838, ADM 92/4, S236, thanking him for a copy of the published logs of the *Great Western*, and wishing him commercial success, and Parry to Claxton, 6 November 1840, ADM 92/4,S420-1, acknowledging reports on the strength of the *Great Western* and asking for any information on 'the large iron ship, including the Screw'.

19 Admiralty to Surveyor, 4 November 1840, ADM 83/25, S5055.

20 Surveyor to Admiralty, 16 November 1840 and 16 January 1841, ADM 92/9, S340 and 413, also endorsement in Minto's hand on the latter. Admiral Sir Charles Adam, First Naval Lord, to Minto, 18 November 1840, NMM, Minto Papers, ELL/228.

21 Parry to Admiralty, 14 December 1840, ADM 92/4, S423-4.

22 Surveyor to Admiralty, 26 February 1841, ADM 92/9,S442.

23 Surveyor to Admiralty, 16 January and 12 February 1841, ADM 92/9, S413 and 432.

24 Parry to Brunel, 22 April 1841, ADM 92/4, S436.

25 Parry to Brunel, 6 and 31 July 1841, ADM 92/4, S445-6 and S446-7.

26 Parry to Brunel, 18 August 1841, ADM 92/4, S448/9.

27 Parry Minute of meeting,sent to the Surveyor, 28 September 1841, ADM 92/4, S453-4.

28 Surveyor to Admiralty, 26 October 1841, ADM 92/10, S165.

29 Admiral Sir Edward Codrington, Commander in Chief, Portsmouth, to Sidney Herbert, First Secretary to the Admiralty, 6 October 1841, Herbert to Codrington, 24 October 1841, NMM, Codrington MSS, COD 17/2 and 20/4.

30 L.T.C. Rolt, *Brunel* (London, 1957), 57; Lady Bourchier, *Memoir of the Life of Admiral Sir Edward Codrington K.C.B.* (London, 1873), Vol. I, 349, Vol. II, 523-4.

31 Codrington to Herbert, 4 August 1843, NMM, Codrington MSS, COD 20/2, 112.

32 Admiralty to Surveyor, 1 January 1842, ADM 83/25, S1928.

33 Admiralty to Symonds, 10 January 1842, with notes by Symonds and Parry of 13 January 1842, ADM 1/5522, S2018.

34 Admiralty to Surveyor, 15 January 1842, ADM 83/25, S2065.

35 Brunel to Admiralty, 10 February 1842, ADM 83/25.

36 Lambert, *Battleships in Transition*, 31-2, concerning the Lisbon trials of 1850 and the success of the screw frigate *Arrogant*.

37 Admiralty to Symonds, 19 February 1842, endorsed in Symonds' hand, 22 February 1842, ADM 1/5522, S2407, and Admiralty to Surveyor, 24 February 1842, endorsed 6 April 1842, ADM 83/25, S2458.

38 Admiralty to Surveyor, 6 April 1842, ADM 83/25, S2895.

39 Surveyor to Captain Superintendent Peter Fisher, at Sheerness, various, April to July 1842, ADM 83/25.

40 Surveyor to Admiralty, 17 January 1842, ADM 92/10, S2156; Rolt, *Brunel*, 286, quoting a letter from Claxton to Brunel's son.

41 Parry to Brunel, 21 May 1842, ADM 92/4, S487-8.

42 Smith to Surveyor, 4 June 1842, ADM 87/12, S3361.

43 Admiralty to Surveyor, 28 July 1842, ADM 83/26, S3942.

44 Admiralty to Brunel, 9 August 1842, ADM 83/26, S4021.

45 Surveyor to Admiralty, 3 September 1842, ADM 92/10, S377.

46 Brunel to Admiralty, 17 September 1842, endorsed by Cockburn, 28 September 1842, ADM 83/27, S4335.

47 Brunel to Admiralty, 20 September 1842, ADM 83/27, S4354.

48 Brunel to Admiralty, 15 October 1842, Maudslay, Son & Field to Admiralty, 12 October 1842, and endorsements, ADM 87/12, S4534; Surveyor to Admiralty, 28 December 1842, ADM 92/10, S429.

49 Rolt, *Brunel*, 286, and D.K. Brown, 'The Introduction of the Screw Propeller into the Royal Navy', *Warship*, No.1, 59-63.

50 Admiralty to Surveyor, 15 January 1842, enclosing Laird to Admiralty, ADM 83/25, S2064.

51 Surveyor to Admiralty, 22 February 1842, ADM 1/5522.

52 Admiralty to Surveyor, 3 May 1842; Blessley to Surveyor, 10 May 1842; F.P. Smith to Admiralty, 31 December 1842; Cockburn Minute, 31 December 1842; Gunley to Admiralty, 21 November 1843, docket given out in February 1846, ADM 83/26, S3143.

53 Ship Propeller Company to Admiralty, 11 June 1842, ADM 87/14, S1372.

54 Cockburn memoranda in Haddington to Peel, 11 June 1845, British Library, Peel Papers, Add. MSS. 40, 458, ff. 55-64. In 1851 *Rattler* was sent to China, and on her return in 1856 was found to be defective and broken up.

55 Cockburn to Captain Sir Charles Napier, 24 October 1844, NMM, Napier MSS, Nap.31.

56 Wood to Minto, 27 January 1843, and Symonds to Minto, 7 January 1845, NMM, Minto Papers, ELL/237.

57 Surveyor to Admiralty, 6 November 1846 and 12 January 1847, criticising the hull form of *Dauntless* and *Arrogant*, ADM 92/12, S295-6. The former was a failure, the latter relatively successful. *Dauntless* was the first attempt to build a full powered screw frigate, *Arrogant* was an auxiliary, her success had more to do with the Penn's trunk engines than any merit in Fincham's hull.

58 Lord Auckland to the Duke of Portland, 7 September 1848, University of Nottingham Library, Portland MSS, PwH 611.

59 Auckland to Rear Admiral Sir Charles Napier, 7 September 1848, British Library, Napier MSS, Add. MSS. 40,023 f.278.

60 For the introduction of steam into the world's battle fleets see, Lambert, *Battleships in Transition*.

61 Basil Greenhill and P. Allington, 'The S.S. *Great Britain* as the World's First Six-Masted Schooner', *Maritime Wales*, No. 9 (1985), 3-28.

62 S. Pollard and P. Robertson, *The British Shipbuilding Industry, 1870-1914* (London, 1979), 15.

63 Sir J. Briggs, *Naval Administrations, 1827-1892* (London, 1897), 67. This work, a source of so many critical remarks, contains many inaccuracies, despite the career of the author. It should be used with great care, and cross referenced. Herbert to Portland, 22 February 1845, University of Nottingham Library, Portland MSS, PwH 810.

64 Auckland to Portland, 17 October 1848, University of Nottingham Library, Portland MSS, PwH 618, which led to the letter referred to in Note 6. It should be emphasised that Auckland's underlying motive in calling for Symonds' opinions was to pacify the Duke of Portland, who was, once again, in a very influential political position.

A SUMMING UP

Ewan Corlett

On behalf of the seminar, I would like to thank both authors for most interesting papers, which have not only provoked much discussion but will lead to further investigation and research. It is quite an achievement to discover a major new screw propelled ship preceding *The Great Britain*, not as large, of course, and which never seemed to have gone into on-going successful service, but which nevertheless blazed a trail and which helped to show the way ahead. Dr. Greenhill must be congratulated on his paper, which will certainly be a source document in the history of screw propulsion.

Dr. Lambert, equally, does much to throw new light upon the events of the 1840s in this field. After his paper there can be no doubt that many of the preconceived ideas regarding the attitude of the Admiralty to screw propulsion must not only be modified but, in some cases, discarded. Brunel does not seem to have been harmed in any way by this research. Rather it is the interpretation of the events by later historians which seems to be at fault. Some of the attitudes ascribed to the Admiralty in general by latter day historians now appear to be quite fallacious, and this is almost disgraceful. This does nothing, however, to diminish the contribution that Brunel as consultant, adviser and father figure made to the successful development, implementation and conclusion of the *Rattler* trials.

I have been invited not only to acknowledge the contribution made by our two authors but also to comment in general on the subjects that they cover.

I must emphasise that the early development of screw propulsion is not only an interesting subject, or indeed even a fascinating one: it is one of great basic importance. The introduction of screw propulsion marked one of the major steps in the progress of mankind. Brunel enunciated the very important principle that 'the resistance of vessels on the water does not increase in direct proportion to the tonnage. The tonnage increases with the cubes of their dimensions while the resistance increases at about their squares ...'. This is correct where wave making effects are not involved or important, and is the origin of the transport efficiency of very large tankers and bulk carriers and, incidentally, of very large aircraft such as the Boeing 747. But not only does the economy of shipping today depend on size but also upon screw propulsion, so the subject of these two papers is of crucial importance. You can say what you like about other means of transport, but for the bulk of the goods moved around the world today, the cost per ton-mile by screw propelled ship is an order of magnitude, i.e. a factor of 10, lower than that of any competitive system.

To introduce the screw propeller as a concept was not enough, nor indeed, later, was the introduction of more efficient engines. Hypothetically, given a more efficient engine, you simply could not apply it. The materials of the day, both of the machinery and of the supporting services such as lubrication, simply were not up to long-distance continuous power propulsion. One could not build a useful compound or triple expansion engine without the boiler pressures and temperatures to provide adequate pressure steam. Similarly, one could not build the boilers without better quality materials, indeed one was really waiting for Bessemer and Siemens-Martin steel to do this.

Efficient engines and high pressure, high temperature steam still would not be enough. Lubricants had to be developed which could cope with high temperatures and high pressures. Animal lubricants in use in the day of *The Great Britain*, e.g. tallow, simply carbonised at these temperatures and pressures, so that efficient high temperature mineral-based lubricants were necessary. The same applied to seals. Rope packing seals lubricated with tallow were not adequate and yet efficient, mechanical spring-loaded seals were invented in the very early days of the nineteenth century, indeed were envisaged as normal good practice in Sir Mark Brunel's triangle engine patent. Again high temperatures and high pressures could not be used if there was any real possibility of lubricant carry-over into boilers, so the jet condenser had to go and efficient surface condensers had to be evolved. These again, were envisaged and had been partially developed in the early nineteenth century, again by people such as Sir Mark Brunel.

Finally, the crucial problem of transmitting the power through a propeller had to be solved. Even if one could supply the necessary torque and revolutions to a propeller shaft over a long period of time this could not be transmitted to the propeller until efficient stern bearings had been developed.

The *Great Eastern* on her maiden voyage to New York wore down her stern bearing by three-quarters of an inch, thus illustrating the magnitude of the problem. Indeed it was this very voyage which led to the development of the water-lubricated lignum vitae stern tube bearing which became the norm for ships for almost the next hundred years.

What I am saying is that the successful introduction of screw propulsion, which itself was responsible for the whole of today's shipping, depended upon an immense infrastructure going back perhaps even to the development of unified screw threads by Whitworth, and early improvements in lathe technology, and certainly the development of better metals and lubricants. It is a fascinating and important subject. It simply has not been researched adequately. Information is available in quantity, but here and there, in dribs and drabs, and not pooled together, correlated and analysed as a whole.

Dare I suggest that this is something that should be attacked by a team who could produce both a valuable and definitive work. The team should consist of four or five people, each of a completely distinctive discipline and each authoritatively knowledgeable in his or her own field. Perhaps I am out of court in floating such an idea while summing up two distinguished papers, but from the few words I have had with both authors I know that they agree and are supportive of the idea, indeed it is partially theirs.

JOHN DELBRIDGE, BARNSTAPLE MERCHANT, 1564-1639

Alison Grant

John Delbridge lived in challenging times. Born in the same year as Shakespeare, he was 24 at the time of the Armada, and not quite 40 when the uneasy reign of James I began. He played a leading part in West Country trade in the years that followed, represented Barnstaple in Parliament, and was one of the earliest promoters of planting and settlement in the New World. He died at the age of 75, three years before the outbreak of the Civil War. This period was a stimulating one for Barnstaple, which had shaken off some ancient restrictions during the Reformation, and secured virtually all manorial rights in 1565. The Corporation thenceforth ruled in the interests of the merchants who controlled it. The town extended its liberties with new charters in 1595 and 1610, but there were still a few battles to win before complete independence was achieved. On a broader front, Barnstaple took part in the campaign against London interests waged at this time by West Country ports for the right to 'free trade', which in those days meant, not lower duties, but the right of any merchant to trade wherever he wished. Delbridge pursued this cause, as he did many others, with dogged determination.

Richard and Alice Delbridge, who were married in Barnstaple in 1557, lost several children in infancy, but reared six daughters, and two sons, of whom John was the elder. As there is no record of Alice Delbridge's maiden name, nothing is known of John Delbridge's connections on his mother's side. His father was a merchant, but not a leading one, and although a member of the corporation, never served as mayor. He did, however, have the means to educate his sons and give them a start as merchants. John Delbridge probably attended Barnstaple grammar school, which had a good record in the sixteenth century. Its most famous scholar was John Jewell, bishop of Salisbury, one of the founders of the Church of England, a man highly revered throughout the country, and especially in north Devon, where he was born and brought up. Jewell had no children; his sister had married Henry Downe, a leading Barnstaple merchant, and in 1585, at the age of 21, John Delbridge married their elder daughter, Agnes.[1] How he made such an advantageous match with a rich merchant's daughter who was also the famous bishop's niece is a matter for conjecture; his father's wealth and status may have been higher than the scanty surviving records indicate, although none of his sisters married particularly well. He may have worked with or for Downe, and have therefore been in a position to woo his daughter, or his strong religious convictions may have recommended him.

John Delbridge was one of 'the hotter sort of protestants' who predominated in the West Country, particularly in the ports, which had long-standing sympathies with the Calvinist Netherlands, and trading connections with the great Huguenot stronghold of La Rochelle. A strongly religious outlook was not inconsistent with a merchant's career and aspirations, for faith could bear him up in adversity, and profits were seen as a reward for virtue and hard work – often regarded as synonymous. This was also the period of 'new learning', and Delbridge and his family respected education, the cloth, and the learned professions. His brother-in-law, John Downe, and his nephew Jonathan Hanmer, both eminent divines, had attended Emmanuel College, Cambridge, and he and his brother both sent their eldest sons there. Nicholas's son, Nathaniel, eventually became a priest, while John's son, John, went on to the Middle Temple, presumably to study law; he died young. Two of Delbridge's sons-in-law, George Hakewill, D.D., and Martin Blake, later vicar of Barnstaple, had studied at Exeter College, Oxford, known for its religious radicalism at the time.[2]

Some members of the establishment felt themselves threatened by religious radicalism; William Cotton, soon after being appointed Bishop of Exeter in 1598, complained bitterly of the 'many clamorous and malicious Rattleheads ... of this Western and turbulent people'. The Earl of Bath, Lord Lieutenant of the county, who lived at Tawstock, near Barnstaple, held the same views, and in 1601 wrote to Robert Cecil, the queen's chief minister, asking him to send the bishop home from London, to deal with the 'seditious schismatics' in the district, and their 'factious and pernicious head', John Delbridge. Delbridge, when mayor, had crossed the Vicar of Barnstaple, who had had more than one brush with the corporation, and the earl was anxious to restore the vicar's position and assert his own jurisdiction over the town. The incident was recorded by the town clerk, Philip Wyot, in his diary:

> Mr Mayor and aldermen, going upon their search in the evening as usual, found the vicar Mr Trender in John Williams' house, being a tippler, with other company, and having among them a pipe with a tabor, a little after nine, and because Mr Trender would not come down to Mr Mayor from the chamber upon commandment ... was committed to ward where he abode till the morning following ....

The vicar, whose eventual epitaph included the text 'many are the troubles of the righteous', 'sent a lamentable letter to the bishop of Exeter', who informed the earl, who at once commanded Delbridge, to come to him at Tawstock. Although the borough court upheld Delbridge's action, saying there was just cause for the vicar to be detained and bound for good behaviour, Delbridge, 'by his honour's persuasion and his own concern remitted to my Lord of Bath's censure'. The vicar had the last laugh, for the 'Sunday following he preached two hours, [and] being a cold day, he wearied all his audience'. Delbridge was, like the town's byelaws, puritanical, but this incident did not make him a schismatic, for he never entertained any notion of breaking away from the Church of England with which his family had such strong connections.[3]

In John Delbridge's time most goods were produced and sold locally, for transport difficulties inhibited the growth of a national market, and even regional ones. Transport by sea, however, meant that ports enjoyed a non-local market area, and were open to news and ideas from other parts of the country, and abroad. Barnstaple was well placed for the Irish and Bristol Channel trades, and for Biscay ports, like La Rochelle and Bilbao. In the sixteenth century old-established trades expanded, and Barnstaple merchants and mariners also took part in new ones, sending ships every year to the Newfoundland fisheries, selling the catch in Spain or Portugal, and returning with Spanish wool and iron from San Sebastion and Bilbao, or olive oil, oranges, wine, and raisins from the south. Barnstaple ships also traded with the 'islands', Madeira, the Canaries, and the Azores, and ventured down the coast of Africa. In 1588, two leading Barnstaple merchants, Richard Dodderidge (whose daughter Delbridge's brother later married), and John Darracott, with six other men from Devon or with Devon connections, formed the first Guinea Company, securing a ten-year monopoly of trade, duty-free, with a coast they had already explored, between the Senegal and Gambia rivers.[4] In this atmosphere of expansion and enterprise, John Delbridge began his career.

Like many aspiring merchants, Delbridge probably served as a factor abroad before his marriage. He does not appear to have traded in his own name before 1590, so he may well have been working with his wife's family at that time. Her uncles, Nicholas and James Downe, were associated with Richard Dodderidge in privateering voyages during the war with Spain, and had a share of the spoils when in 1590, Dodderidge's ship *Prudence*, 100 tons, brought back a Portuguese prize, the *Spiritu Sancto*, 130 tons, from the coast of Guinea, 'having in her four chests of gold to the value of £16,000, and divers chains of gold with civet and other things of great value ... '. During the next two years the *Prudence* brought back three more prizes, one of them worth £10,000. Even if no fall-out from these ventures came Delbridge's way the example was not lost on him, for in 1596, the town clerk's diary records, '... came to the Quay head an old ship of Mr John Delbridge's called the *Busse* of 120 tons to reprisal abroad'. There is no record that this vessel took any prizes, so it was fortunate that her owner was now established as a merchant.[5]

By the 1590s, Delbridge had acquired enough status and capital (or credit) to join the cloth-traders, exporting mainly Barnstaple bays, which, cheaper and lighter than the traditional kerseys and broadcloths, sold well in Spain and France. In 1591 he sent out six cargoes, all to La Rochelle, which as an entrepôt for Spanish goods, supplied him with return cargoes of Spanish wool, as well as French canvas, which was used for wrapping bales of cloth. He also imported 100 stone of Irish wool from Cork, and took part in the coastal trade, shipping 'wine of Madeira' and other goods to Bristol. A few years later, he had enlarged the scope of his trade, importing Newfoundland train oil in his own ship, the *Busse*, wine and sugar from the Canary Islands, and quantities of Spanish wool and iron, which, when war made direct trade with Spain difficult, came by way of La Rochelle, or Bayonne and St. Jean de Luz, close to the border.[6]

Like most successful Barnstaple merchants, John Delbridge became a member of the corporation. He showed leadership when, during a food shortage in 1596, he helped to convince the members that they would have to find the money for 'a whole ship's lading'. When this was exhausted, he was one of two members who bought rye to sell to the poor at a low price to relieve a serious situation. His prompt and sympathetic action at this time probably made an impression, for it was not long before he was elected mayor. As the town's interests expanded, its mayor sometimes had to travel, usually to Exeter to meet representatives of other Devon towns, and occasionally farther afield. In May 1601, the town clerk complained that no dinner was kept at the mayor's house on one of the sessions days, 'Mr John Delbridge, mayor, being absent in Northamptonshire or London on business ...'. On the borders of Northamptonshire stood Burghley House, which had been built by Elizabeth's chief minister, and inherited, like the position, by his son, Robert Cecil. This was almost certainly the man with whom Delbridge had business in Northamptonshire or London.[7]

Among other matters, Cecil may have wanted to discuss the transport of troops to Ireland, from Barnstaple, which was an important port of embarkation for Elizabethan and later campaigns there. Delbridge's job was to hire and provision ships for men and horses, and advance the money to despatch them. He completed this work after his term as mayor ended, and in November 1601 sent a letter to the Privy Council to say that the latest draft of close on 1000 men had sailed from north Devon. The letter is endorsed, 'Haste, haste, post haste. Exeter at past 12 of the clock. Honiton at past five at afternoon. Sherborne at 12 in the night. Sarum past 9 before noon. Andover at 6 at night. Hertford Bridge [Staines] at 7 in the morning'. The news thus took only about 48 hours to reach the capital. Delbridge probably continued to discuss important matters with Cecil in London or elsewhere, and to send post boys and horses galloping through the night with urgent letters, for at about this time he became one of the minister's agents in the South West.[8]

In wartime, England's early warning system relied on reports by incoming vessels, with West Country mariners often first home with the news. Delbridge was now part of Cecil's information network, and in 1602, for instance, wrote to him with news from the Azores:

A Barnstaple ship reports before leaving Terceira Island, letters had arrived there from the King of Spain saying that a fleet of 300 Flemings was bound for that place, requiring them to defend themselves and promising aid, so they are busy mustering men, victualling castles, making trenches etc. There are only 3-400 soldiers at Terceira, and none at St. Michael's.

A few months later he sent news from nearer home: 'Last night a bark from Ireland arrived at Ilfracombe, reporting the landing of the Spaniards in Ireland. I sent a friend to know the truth, and enclose his reply.'[9]

Mariners, merchants, messengers, and probably most of the people of Barnstaple knew that Delbridge was working for Cecil, so he was hardly a secret agent, but he was involved in a little undercover work, with the help of his factor, William Palmer, whom he described as 'my man in St. Jean de Luz'. In 1604, for instance, he was able to inform Cecil, 'I hear from Palmer ... that the French King has sent an ambassador to the King of Spain. The Spaniards are gathering companies in Castile and Andalusia, and purchasing ships. They hear of a fleet preparing in England, and so have sent two ships to the Groyne, to run on our coast and learn its proceedings ...'. Palmer's letters to agents in Spain are apparently concerned with selling goods, yet they survive among Cecil's state papers. He promised to send a Scots agent in Valladolid some russet stockings, for instance, and asked for his help in securing a licence to send Barnstaple bays into Spain, adding, '... my master, John Delbridge, is at the Court of England about the same matter'. Provincial merchants not infrequently took trade matters to the Privy Council, but Delbridge may also have been in London for other reasons. The russet stockings crop up again in another of Palmer's letters to Valladolid, this time to an Italian, Jeronimo Paluzzi. A hint of cloak and dagger can be detected here, for Palmer asked him to send his reply 'in a cover' via another agent in San Sebastian. He warned Paluzzi, 'I pray you, do not write ... of any acquaintance that my master has with your great friend', and went on, 'Touching your bill of exchange ... my master writes that he has received the same and sent it to your great friend.' Paluzzi's great friend and paymaster was presumably Cecil, and Palmer and his master, John Delbridge, were links in a chain by which the minister kept in touch with these agents.[10]

Delbridge's work for Cecil, which continued after the end of the war, nettled the Earl of Bath, who felt his position was being undermined, for he reckoned it part of the Lord Lieutenant's duties to send local information to the government. At this time, the nobility, who had lost much ground in central government, were clinging tenaciously to local power, while towns like Barnstaple aimed to control their own affairs. The earl, a rather weak man, had recently lost a quarrel with Exeter, and feared further humiliation if he failed to control affairs in the town nearest to his home. Although he had quarrelled with Barnstaple long before Delbridge became mayor, the earl regarded him as the most radical of his opponents after 1600, and bombarded Cecil with blistering attacks on 'your servant John Delbridge who glories in his opposition with me in many things'. Whether or not he gloried in it, Delbridge's opposition was scarcely surprising, for the earl was doing all in his power to wreck the 'New Work', a scheme to extend Barnstaple Quay.[11]

The New Work began in 1600 with a 'new quay upon the Strand, almost in the midst of the other quay'. When a deep hole was dug on part of the site in 1981, many sherds of late sixteenth-century pottery came to light, probably part of the 'back-fill' behind the new line of the quay, and indicative of reclamation at about that time. The town undertook the work on the quay, and Delbridge leased and enclosed the newly-gained plot, 126 feet by 80, and erected houses and other buildings on it. He also got permission to build an 'appentice [penthouse] ... against the long wall of the said New Work next adjoining the quay and highway, and ... receive the profit thereof ... of such as shall there set up any standings or sell any wares or merchandises whatsoever in the Market days or otherwise during the said term'.[12] Development such as this was typical of ports in this expanding period, providing facilities for those who brought goods by land and water to buy and sell on the quayside.

Alleging that the new quay obstructed navigation, the Earl of Bath, as Vice-Admiral of Devon, began proceedings in the Admiralty Court, securing the verdict 'that it was noisome to passage of boats and barges'. The town saw this as unwarranted interference in its affairs, and briefed lawyers to fight the indictment that followed. The matter dragged through the courts for years, and Delbridge sought help from the Privy Council, which, although it expressed its 'great regard for the town of Barnstaple', failed in its attempt to mediate. After 'much ado at the Assizes', the verdict went against the town, which, however, got the case re-opened. Both sides now procured boatmen to say that the New Work did, or did not, hinder their passage of the bridge. At last 'Mr Delbridge's side' produced the more convincing boatman, and the judges 'then well thought that [the] matter was carried against the town of malice and displeasure, so there they award that this business should go no farther'. In 1608 the Earl of Bath's lawyers began a new complaint, and Delbridge's lease of 1609, for which he paid £100, bore an escape clause to cover him should 'part or portion of the premises ... within four years next, by the due course of the law of this realm ... be ordered ... to be thrown down ...'. In the end nothing was 'thrown down', and 24 years later, the town allowed Delbridge to renew his lease free of charge, being especially moved, as they said, 'in consideration of the great suits and charges in law which the said John Delbridge hath expended and been put into about ... the building of the premises, by the tenants of the Right Honourable the Earl of Bath ... pretending the said building to be a hindrance unto and for the passage of barges ...'. That particular Right Honourable Earl of Bath was dead by then, but such a mark of appreciation for John Delbridge, then in his seventieth year, would have been enough to make the earl turn in his splendid tomb in Tawstock Church![13]

The Earl of Bath nominated one, and in practice sometimes both, of Barnstaple's M.P.s, refusing to consider names put forward by the town, and in 1597, had even forced a new election when the freemen dared to vote in one of their own number.[14] After enduring the earl's opposition to the New Work for ten years, however, the town was no longer subservient, and in 1610 returned John Delbridge, now its acknowledged leader. He was a good choice, for he was prepared to stand up for the town's interests, had friends in high places, and, although the town sometimes granted a few pounds towards his 'charges' as M.P., was able to pay the lion's share of his expenses. He represented Barnstaple in every parliament over the next nineteen years. His speeches reveal his character, his concerns, and a lively oratorical style. 'Trade is much decayed and lieth a-bleeding', he proclaimed in 1621, when a severe depression was seriously affecting the manufacture of cloth. Delbridge, a cloth merchant, spoke of its dire effects in Barnstaple; instead of 'a thousand pair of looms in Barnstaple, [and] many thousand people; not 200 looms, not now 200', he declared. He believed the depression was deepened by restrictions on trade, especially the 'impositions' recently added to customs duties. As one of only a handful of merchant M.P.s he played an active part in debates on trade, and the government's indifference brought an outburst from him at the end of the session. 'We have been here 16 weeks,' he protested, 'and in the matter of trade, nothing has been done. I had rather never have gone home than go home in this manner. I do dislike it, I protest it will do that hurt, I wish I were in heaven.'[15]

In the debate that followed, Delbridge crossed swords with Lionel Cranfield, one of the king's ministers, who, armed with statistics supplied by customs officers, told him that Barnstaple's trade was as great as in Elizabeth's time, and the trouble was caused by imports exceeding exports. Delbridge retorted that the customs returns concealed a threefold rise in duties, adding, 'We cannot send out £100 in goods but homewards and outwards we pay £25 to the king; perchance the merchant may get £5 for himself, a poor reward considering the adventure ... I had rather be a ploughman than a merchant.' Cranfield's continued attempts to crush his opponent aroused the sympathy of the House for the West Country merchant, so the minister had to give ground, at least in the matter of free trade, an issue which had been keenly fought by West Country M.P.s in all James I's parliaments. When Cranfield finally promised, 'Let the burgesses of the Outports make never so much Haste into the Country, there will be Order taken before they come home, for their Ease and Liberty of Free Trade'. This was a considerable victory; as one of Delbridge's supporters remarked at the end of the debate, 'after six windy days, a fair evening!'[16]

When parliament was urging the king to send troops to help his protestant son-in-law, the Elector Palatine, against catholic invaders, Delbridge, always an emotional speaker, became quite theatrical in the protestant cause, proclaiming, 'I will be as forward as any shall be, and be ready to go in person.' His offer was probably meant seriously, but was hardly practical, for he was 56 years old, and his military experience was probably limited to the local militia. His valour was not put to the test, for James I, maintaining his prerogative to decide foreign policy, did not follow parliament's advice. He also refused to allow a debate on his plan to marry the heir to the throne to the Infanta of Spain, rejected parliament's petition on the subject, and arrested some of its leaders. The Commons, outraged at this violation of privilege, convened in silence, no-one daring to broach the matters uppermost in everyone's mind. At last Delbridge got up and began to speak on West-Country trade, but affected by the charged atmosphere, changed tack, and gave the lead for which M.P.s had been waiting. 'Let us leave trade and impositions, and speak for religion and the privileges of this House,' he cried, 'let us petition and petition again as we usually do to God, and without ceasing till he hear us.' He knew the king was determined to suppress 'fiery and turbulent spirits' in the House, but declared he would rather risk royal anger than catholic domination – or as he put it himself, 'I would as willingly hang under a gallows as fry over a faggot.' He and many of his hearers could remember the Armada and the Gunpowder Plot, and to them papists and Spaniards were perpetual enemies of the realm. The next day, saying that some people had taken him to task for his speech, he asked to be cleared by a vote of the House. M.P.s rallied to his support, and gave him what amounted to a vote of confidence. The outspoken member for Barnstaple was playing his part in the affairs of the nation.[17]

The king soon dissolved this refractory parliament, but many of the same M.P.s were returned to the next in 1624, which ended with prayers and fasting for the protestants of La Rochelle, once again at war with the King of France. The new king, Charles I, alienated many M.P.s by his marriage to the French princess,

Henrietta Maria, and his promise to tolerate English catholics. In the closing debate of the next parliament, Delbridge spoke, as he so often did, with the voice of the man in the street, or at least of the middle-class trader in a West-Country port, when he complained of 'nothing but discouragements, pardons to Jesuits, the news from Rochelle ... the interruption of the fishing trade, the losses by pirates; so that whereas we returned the last time with fasting and prayer, now we may return with sackcloth and ashes.' A few years later, however, he opposed war with France, even on behalf of La Rochelle. Like many M.P.s, he had clamoured for war with Spain, but the ill-organised Cadiz expedition had such adverse effects in the South West, that he and other West-Country M.P.s felt it would be disastrous to send similar expeditions to La Rochelle.[18] They spoke from knowledge of the difficulties of collecting money and fitting out ships, but were outvoted. The demand for two ships to be provided and provisioned by Barnstaple for another expedition was the last straw. In opposing help for the protestants now undergoing a terrible siege in La Rochelle, Delbridge was abandoning his oft-stated principles, but in the event the two English expeditions to relieve the port did more harm than good, so at least he had shown good practical sense in opposing them.

In the parliament of 1628, M.P.s, conveniently forgetting that they had granted far too little money for the wars they had advocated, bitterly attacked unparliamentary taxation, particularly the forced loan of 1627 imposed on all subsidy men (taxpayers), after which many were 'daily imprisoned for refusing to lend to the king'.[19] Devon and Cornwall had their own grievance, for scandalously undisciplined, unpaid, unfed, underclad, and plague-ridden troops were still billeted in the two counties many months after their return from Cadiz. When parliament met, M.P.s were determined to seek redress of grievances before granting the king money. John Delbridge joined in the attack, incidentally painting a grim picture of the distress caused in Devon by the recent wars:

No county pays so much subsidy as Devonshire. Their trade gave them the means which is now dead; trade into France and Spain, then their fishing in Newfoundland .... The chief reason of enriching the country [meaning county] is gone, which was fishing. £100,000 a year came in thither by fishing. All things are dead with us, and yet we are called upon to give.... [People's] monies taken from them, not to be called a loan, when a pursuivant stood by them to carry them away that refused. Soldiers billetted amongst them, a great charge.... The poor town I serve paid £700 in a little time for soldiers.... Soldiers and pursuivants are now our companions, and although in the poor towns where the labourer lives by his trade, he offers his goods to be sold to pay for these billettings, yet nothing will satisfy but ready money.[20]

The king, desperate for a grant from parliament, at last agreed to the Petition of Right, which listed what the Commons described as 'murdering grievances'. Delbridge's proposal to include impositions was outvoted, but forced loans and other unparliamentary taxation, arbitrary imprisonment, billetting, and martial law were checked.[21]

Like many M.P.s, John Delbridge served on committees on subjects in which he had special knowledge. One was concerned with poldavy (sailcloth), and another with new draperies. West-Country M.P.s needed to be well-represented when cloth was under discussion, for they had fought a long campaign against the efforts of London-based companies to monopolise its export. It was probably the leader of the free trade 'lobby', Sir Edwin Sandys, who had interests in many new trading enterprises, who inspired Delbridge to widen his commercial horizons. It is noticeable that the most enterprising provincial merchants in the early seventeenth century were M.P.s, for their parliamentary duties brought them to London, which offered exciting new opportunities and contacts. Delbridge's career as a merchant blossomed after 1610, when he entered parliament. In 1611, he became one of the few Devon members of the East India Company, and the only one from Barnstaple. This may only have involved investing capital, but he perhaps also gained some opportunities to buy and sell goods. By 1621, however, he had sold £300 worth of 'old East India Company stock', and probably did not keep up his membership thereafter.[22]

John Delbridge must have been a wealthy man when he bought his East India stock. The ten or twelve years after the end of war with Spain, in 1604, had been good years for trade, and from this time onwards Delbridge also invested in property, much of which he rented out. He had several properties in Barnstaple, and a small country house at Rumsam, about a mile outside the town, possibly inherited from his father who died there in 1608. In 1611, he paid £1800 for the title to the manor of West Buckland, with the manor house, barton, and farm, and later leased more land there, and in many other parishes around Barnstaple.[23] With these safe investments behind him, he could afford to risk some more exciting projects, and within a couple of years had joined more trading companies. He may have become a member of the North West Passage Company, in the hope that exploration of northern waters would open up new fishing grounds, but of more immediate importance was the Virginia Company of London, which Delbridge joined in 1612, just as tobacco was beginning to transform the economy of the colony.[24]

Two Virginia Companies had been founded in 1606, the Plymouth Company under Sir Ferdinando Gorges, to settle lands north of 38 degrees N., and the London Company, which gained the lands to the south, including what became the colony of Virginia. Delbridge joined the London Company, probably at the instigation of Sandys, who was one of the leading promoters. Some members were interested only in investment, but Delbridge, who never seems to have held more than three of the £12 10s. shares, wanted to build up trade, which involved setting up a plantation and sending out settlers. This was an integral part of colonization in the early seventeenth century, for apart from furs and fish, there was little to send home without settlers to exploit natural resources or grow cash crops. Although London finance dominated the Company, many great merchants did not want to be involved in planting, so there was room for a provincial entrepreneur. In 1616 the Company granted 50 acres of land with each share bought. This was soon increased to 100 acres, with an extra 50 for every person transported to work the shareholder's estate. Delbridge applied for a patent for a 'particular plantation', and in November

1619, was given permission to transport 200 people. Four months later the *Swan* of Barnstaple, 100 tons, sailed with the first 71, 'choice men ... out of Devonshire ... brought up to Husbandry'. All survived the voyage, and the Company resolved that 'some other ships might be sent out of Barnstaple by the help of Mr Delbridge'. Delbridge's importance in the early development of the colony was acknowledged when, in 1621, he was made a member of His Majesty's Council for Virginia, a unique achievement for a provincial trader.[25]

In 1609, when Sir George Somer's flagship, *Sea Venture*, was driven aground on Bermuda after being separated by a storm from a fleet sailing for Virginia, the London Virginia Company acquired an interest in the island. A few years later it sold its rights to an offshoot, the Somers Islands Company, which allocated land to its shareholders on condition that they sent out settlers. Delbridge was soon established in the emigration 'trade', and in 1619, promised to send to Bermuda 30 or 40 'honest, painful [painstaking], labour men etc, poor hard-working boys or girls which may do good service', for Sir Edwin Sandys and other prominent members of the Company, aboard the *Pelican* of Barnstaple, 80 tons. Pointing out the 'extraordinary' cost of sending a ship to Bermuda, as 'our owners and mariners are fearful of that place, being ever reported a place very dangerous', he said he would need to charge £5 per head for passages, or be 'in hazard to lose'. Delbridge also intended to send some settlers of his own, four heifers and a bull, provisions for the voyage, and 'some quantity of meal and bread' for the emigrants to land with them, all aboard a vessel which would have been scarcely 50 feet on the keel. The *Pelican* had previously been in the Newfoundland trade, but Delbridge described her as 'a ship most fit for passage of people', so she probably had two decks, between which passengers could be accommodated with about 4' 6" headroom. Even so, she was very much larger than the small vessels he sent out later.[26]

John Delbridge's small ships did much to establish and maintain settlement in Bermuda. The vessel he sent in 1620 was again 'freighted mainly with passengers', most of them 'well-chosen labouring boys for apprentices, for which she came to a good market'. The London 'Magazine' ship arrived late that year, having lost 20 or 30 of her emigrants on the voyage, 'ten persons ... taken out of Newgate' being thought to be the source of the infection. Her other passengers were also unsuitable, being ladies and gentlemen of fashion. They, and those who sent them, were more interested in profit than the welfare of the colony, and grudged Delbridge's small ship her homeward cargo of 10,000 lbs of tobacco, although the Magazine vessel took a full lading of 60,000 lbs. With the islanders, however, Delbridge's ships were popular, and their arrival an event worth recording. In 1621:

Appeareth upon the coast a small ship of Barnstaple in the west country of England belonging to one Mr Delbridge, a brother of the Somers Islands Company, and wholly set out by himself. She came into the town's harbour and was very well conditioned, and with her a convenient and well-chosen magazine ... the most part of [which] ... was sold to the inhabitants, the remainder thereof being afterwards to be carried to Virginia. By this bark also are brought some few more inhabitants, as likewise single women to sell for wives and young boys for apprentices.[27]

In return for free passages, poor emigrants were formally apprenticed for a term of years before sailing, and it was established practice for merchants and others to sell their indentures to the highest bidder on arrival. Delbridge obviously had no qualms about separating youngsters from their families, or shipping young women from the lower orders into the unknown as 'maids for wives'; it would hardly have occurred to him or any other seventeenth-century merchant that he was exploiting such people. He treated his human cargo well by the standards of the day, and they, with no higher expectations, may even have been grateful.

The Company soon limited trade to London ships, and condemned Delbridge as an 'interloper'. When this failed to stop him, they demanded a payment of £2 for every passenger brought in, and 2d. on every pound of tobacco shipped out, instructing the Governor to lay these charges on his goods. Delbridge, still hoping to obtain trade rights, agreed in 1626 to pay £200 for 'an acquittance of all manner of actions, suits, quarrels, debts, sum and sums of money due to the Company from the beginning of the world to date'. A less persevering man might well have given up, for at this time he also lost £300 when the master of the *Olive* of Bideford, 30 tons, literally failed to find Bermuda, arriving back in Barnstaple after almost eight months at sea. Plenty of provisions remained, but with no anti-scorbutics, the mariners were 'all sick and weak' and three of the passengers had died. Delbridge was sad at their loss. He wrote, 'I have found it by experience that having sent divers times small ships both to Virginia and Bermuda, and that full of people, I never lost man woman or child going or coming before this last voyage.' In spite of the three deaths, his record was probably unequalled in the period.[28]

In 1627 Delbridge agreed to send no more ships to Bermuda without the Company's consent, but pointed out that he had already despatched the *Olive* to make good her abortive voyage of the previous year. When the Company refused to accept this, he protested that he sold 'better pennyworths' that his London competitors, and that having provided a ship 'with necessaries for the poor planters', including 'at least a hundred poor souls' he had himself sent out, he would continue to send them provisions, even if he was not allowed to bring home tobacco. Although there was obviously profit in supplying settlers' needs, it seems fair to assume that Delbridge did feel some responsibility towards the people he had sent. They rallied to his support, maintaining that he 'supplied at reasonable rates necessaries of which there was great dearth, and dealt fairly with the colonists who ventured a few pounds of tobacco with him'.[29]

The extent of the Bermuda settlers' dependence on Delbridge's supplies was shown the next year when the Company ordered the Governor to prevent islanders trading with Delbridge's ships. He had, of course, already sent one, and its arrival in November 1628, produced petitions from every tribe (division) of the island claiming that the 'prohibiting of the good ship of Barnstaple to discharge herself of her lading', would leave the people 'frustrated of the benefit they do expect and which formerly they have received in times of scarcity by the ships sent from thence.' Pleading that they were destitute of provisions, and especially of corn, and that if the ship were sent away prices would rise beyond their power to pay, the settlers begged the Governor to allow 'Mr Delbridge's factors free leave to trade ... whereby your petitioners may at some easier rates provide for themselves and families.' The Governor capitulated, and allowed Delbridge's ship to discharge and sell her cargo. The master, Benjamin Delbridge, son of John Delbridge's brother Nicholas, then respectfully requested a modest lading of 6,000 lbs of tobacco homeward, which the Island's Council passed with only one dissentient voice, that of the governor. The next year, although instructed by the governor to await a second Company ship, the same Council allowed Delbridge's ship to take 30,000 lbs, fearing that if the London vessel did not turn up, they would have no market for the late crop. The knowledge that Delbridge planned his voyages to collect this late cargo, 'stimulated the islanders to tardiness', as one governor wrote, for they preferred to deal with the Barnstaple merchant, whom they trusted to carry out commissions for them, as well as buy and sell fairly.[30]

London interests not only dominated the Somers Islands Company, but secured a series of royal proclamations decreeing that tobacco could only be imported through the capital. Attempts at evasion brought a government crackdown. In 1629, a King's Messenger was sent 'to fetch up the person of John Delbridge', to answer a charge of refusing to pay duties, and encouraging others to do likewise. The Privy Council, however, found 'that the same complaint was false', and decreed that his accusers should pay his costs. More trouble occurred in 1631, when a ship returned from Bermuda damaged. Delbridge got the Barnstaple customs officers to certify that it was too leaky to send to London according to the proclamation, and therefore the tobacco had been taken out because it was 'likely to perish if not cared for'. The authorities, doubting this, ordered him to send the cargo to London at his own expense, and when he appealed, went to the length of ordering a ship and seamen to be pressed to 'send it to London by sea or to Bristol and overland, taking care that none be embezzled, but that all be delivered unto H.M.'s storehouses at his Custom House in London'. Delbridge responded with a petition, but this was eventually turned down by the Privy Council.[31]

John Delbridge must often have wondered whether his returns were worth the tribulations he endured, and there are signs that he lost in the end. Even good cargoes, like the 13,120 lbs of Bermuda tobacco, brought back by the *Olive* in 1628, and valued by customs at £3280, may not have made him much profit, for not only had he had to buy and transport the product, but the selling price fluctuated with quality and the market, and was often less than the customs valuation, on which duties were based. When he complained in parliament that tobacco duties could amount to over 75 per cent of the selling price, he was probably speaking from bitter experience. The wars with Spain and France added to merchants' problems, and when Delbridge applied for a letter of marque to set out the *John* of Barnstaple as a privateer, he claimed to be seeking reprisal for losses of £10,000. No reliance can be placed on such figures but as some owners listed lesser sums, and some none, Delbridge probably did suffer wartime losses. A reprisal ship, which cost a good deal to set out, was a gamble which might literally bring home a big prize; in the event, the *John* brought none.[32]

In his trade with Virginia, John Delbridge again encountered opposition from London interests, and he ceased to attend meetings of the Virginia Company. The Company, split by internal quarrels, neglected settlers' needs, and in the year after the massacre of 1622, in which almost 350 were killed by Indians, sent no supplies to the survivors, who, having lost homes, stores and crops, were suffering from a serious food shortage. It was fortunate for them that Delbridge, ignoring the London monopoly, despatched a number of Barnstaple ships to Virginia with fish, which was all quickly sold in a land almost 'destitute of food'. A letter sent to him from a factor in Virginia at this time listed several ships by name, including the *Success*, whose voyage illustrates the extensive range of Delbridge's colonial trade. Having already completed a fishing voyage in northern waters and sailed down the coast to Virginia, she went on to Bermuda, and arrived back in Barnstaple with '7566 lbs weight of Bermudas tobacco value £1491 10s., for John Delbridge, merchant'. Delbridge sent some of the tobacco abroad, and a good deal to Ireland, bringing back Irish wool for the local cloth industry. The cloth was then exported to La Rochelle, whence came cargoes of French salt for the fishing vessels he and his brother sent to Newfoundland or New England.[33]

The *Success* probably reached Barnstaple before the letter from Virginia, which was written after she sailed, and addressed 'to the Worshipful John Delbridge, Merchant in Barnstaple by way of Canada', showing that some other Barnstaple vessel was returning by another route. The word Canada embraced a vast amount of undefined northern territory, where Barnstaple ships were now exploiting offshore fishing grounds. In later years ships from Boston and other northern ports sent provisions to the southern colonies, but in the years before New England was established, West-Country fishing vessels, particularly those of Barnstaple, pioneered this trade. Delbridge may have had such long-distance trading voyages in mind when he set up his Virginia plantation, for in 1619, a meeting of the directors of the Company heard that Mr John Delbridge, purposing to settle a particular colony in Virginia, desired of the Company that for the defraying of some part of his charges that he might be admitted to fish at Cape Cod. As Sir Ferdinando Gorges refused to allow the southern company any jurisdiction over the rich fishing grounds off New England, Delbridge had to negotiate with the northern company. He seems to have obtained the privileges he desired by offering to check unauthorised vessels, for in 1622, the Council for New England inquired into 'what course Mr Delbridge of Barnstaple taketh against any touching abuses done in New England', and found that he had taken out a warrant against five master mariners from north Devon. Another five were also listed but later crossed out. They had perhaps compounded their offences, for one or two of them were among the masters of Barnstaple vessels granted fishing licences a few months later. The owners and masters probably owed this concession to Delbridge, who had so long sought it.[34]

The Council for New England was now trying to encourage settlement, and Delbridge is likely to have been one of the group of Barnstaple merchants who, in 1623, were negotiating a grant 'for settling a plantation in New England' on payment of £250. There is no record that this plantation was ever set up, nor do any details survive of the grant Delbridge got eight years later to establish a plantation of his own. It is obvious, however, from the cargoes of the vessels which sailed annually from north Devon to New England in the 1630s, that settlements were being set up and supplied. The cargo carried by the 160-ton *Providence* of Barnstaple, for example, one of five ships sent in 1636, was:

98 young bullocks alias yearlings
12 mantles and 4 coats
8 dozen pairs Irish stockings

Vessels leaving the port of Barnstaple in these years also carried emigrants, and it is significant that by the end of the decade, a settlement called Barnstable had been founded on Cape Cod. John Delbridge, although not its actual founder, had done more than anyone else from old Barnstaple to secure fishing rights, establish trade, and promote emigration to New England. Through the inter-colonial trade which his enterprises generated, many small north Devon vessels had become familiar with the coasts of North America in the 1620s and 30s. Barnstaple's Customs Officer respectfully described Delbridge as 'freeman of the Society of Bermuda and Virginia'; his pioneering work helped to make the masters and mariners of the small vessels he sent freemen of the North Atlantic.[35]

John Delbridge's struggle for the freedom of small provincial vessels to trade wherever they could was significant in a town that had its own battles against central control. When there was no parliament, opposition could be repressed, and in 1640, the year after Delbridge's death, Barnstaple was fined £100 in the Star Chamber, '*pro falso clamore*', presumably for airing anti-government views. Eight years earlier, probably for a similar reason, Delbridge and Pentecost Dodderidge, who had served as his fellow M.P., had been haled before the Court of Exchequer. The Corporation paid their fines and expenses, and subsequently made Delbridge, then in his seventy-fifth year, mayor for the third time. They recognised his services by granting him a number of leases free of charge, in consideration of:

the great pains, travels and expenses which the said John Delbridge hath been at for the credit and good of the said borough and town of Barnstaple, being a Burgess at every Parliament since the seventh year of ... King James ..., and in respect that the said John Delbridge hath taken divers journeys unto London and at court for the only [sole] business of the said Town and for his care therein.

This unique compliment shows how much Delbridge had made the town's cause his own.[36]

One of Delbridge's journeys to London on the town's behalf was for an interview with the Lord Keeper in 1632, in an attempt to get the government to act against 'Turkish' pirates who were threatening trade routes in the Atlantic. He then took it upon himself to write to the mayors of West-Country seaports, requesting vigorous action, for otherwise these raiders would 'fall upon our fishing ships both at Newfoundland and Virginia [here meaning New England]', and capture ships and men. Shortly afterwards Delbridge and representatives from five other western ports drew up a list of resolutions, and agreed to petition the king. They were hoist with their own petard when, two years later, Charles I levied ship money to enable him to put down these pirates. Ports were used to such writs in wartime, but a peacetime demand was a different matter. Barnstaple, however, did not object on principle but to the amount of the levy, £250 in 1634, which certainly seems excessive, as Plymouth was only asked for £185, and Bideford a mere £40. Although subsequent writs were scaled down, there was smouldering discontent when ship money became an annual event. John Hampden, who as an ex-M.P. would have been known to Delbridge, lost his famous case against ship money, but the fact that five of the twelve royal judges found for him, encouraged others to withhold payments, not least in Barnstaple, where it took strenuous efforts to collect the levy of 1637. The half dozen who stood firm in their refusal included Delbridge himself, assessed at £3, Richard, his son, at 10s., Martin Blake, his son-in-law who owed 15s., and Mary Delbridge, probably another relation. It looked as if Delbridge would once more be called to account for refusing to pay dues and encouraging others to follow his example, for the defaulters were told to pay, or appear before the Privy Council. Mary Delbridge may have paid her three shillings, for her name was not on the final list. Richard Delbridge said he would make answer to the Council. Martin Blake, who was Vicar of Barnstaple, sent in a long remonstrance to the Bishop of Exeter. John Delbridge neither paid nor faced the consequences; perhaps he got the last laugh, for he died before the matter was resolved.[37]

There are a good many public records of John Delbridge's work, but no private letters or diaries, and no portrait, so glimpses of the man himself are rare. A defendant in a law-suit said Delbridge had spoken to him in Barnstaple 'in a smiling and jesting manner', so he was not always the stern man of duty who had objected to the vicar's tippling; he even counted an alehouse among the properties he leased! Always the businessman, his words to the man he smiled at were, 'You are a debtor of mine', but he did wait for many years before taking him to court. Although a thorn in the flesh of the wealthy and influential men he crossed, he won respect and gratitude from many others. As a member of the Corporation, M.P., and even as employer and entrepreneur, he had shown consideration for the poor, and for people like seamen, settlers, and taxpayers as well as fellow-merchants, and others who benefited from the battles he fought for free trade, free fishing, free speech and other rights. He won a reputation as an honest trader with those who dealt with him at home and abroad, but where unwelcome regulations were concerned, he was wily, for he seldom met his rivals head on. Although he would have used a more elegant turn of phrase to express it, his attitude to the great companies that controlled trade was, 'if you can't beat 'em, join 'em', for as a member he could demand equality of treatment, express surprise if he did not receive it, and negotiate to gain time. If his rivals attempted to stop his voyages, he heard of it after the ships had left port; if cargoes were landed at Barnstaple instead of London, it was always for some reason beyond his control – obviously act of God! He played this commercial chess on the Atlantic board for many years, sacrificing some pieces but taking others; and although he did not win every match, he proved himself a grand master.

John Delbridge's will was a modest one; he left only £5, for instance, to the poor of Barnstaple, although he had earlier given his house in Barnstaple to endow a charity in memory of his elder daughter. Apart from prudent investments in land, much of it held in trust for his heirs, there seems to have been little left to show for his years of enterprise, a fact which his colleagues on the Corporation had probably been aware of when they granted him new leases without charge. He had suffered other blows; of the four of his children who grew up, two died before him. He was, however, probably gratified that his surviving son achieved the status of a gentleman, and married into the Chichester family. Other Barnstaple merchants of his day are remembered by the almshouses or other charities they founded, or their impressive monuments in the church, but, lacking these tangible memorials Delbridge is almost forgotten. If his reputation rested on his local and parliamentary work alone, he would rank as the most prominent townsman of his day, but his most outstanding achievements were in colonial trade and settlement. If Delbridge had a vision of Empire, there is no record of it, but his knowledge of trade, ships and voyages, of the kind of people needed for settlement, and the goods needed to sustain them, enabled him to play a greater practical part in planting and maintaining colonies than any other provincial merchant and many London entrepreneurs. His determined efforts to gain a place in New World trade for himself, the town of Barnstaple and West-Country interests in general, earned him the nickname of 'the Free Trader' on both sides of the Atlantic – a fitting tribute for a man described by a noted American historian as 'probably the most influential and important of all the West-Country merchants'.[38]

NOTES

1   T. Wainwright, ed., *Barnstaple Parish Register 1538-1812* (Exeter, 1903), Marriages, 4; North Devon Record Office (hereafter NDRO), North Devon Athenaeum Collection (hereafter NDA), 3973, 31; J.J. Howard, ed., *Miscellanea Genealogica and Heraldica*, 3rd series, I (1896), 200.

2   *Dictionary of National Biography*, Downe, Hakewill, Hanmer; J. Venn and J.A. Venn, eds, *Alumni Cantabrigiensis*, Pt.II, Vol. II, 30; J.F. Chanter, *The Life and Times of Martin Blake, B.D.* (1910), 13.

3   R.J.E. Boggis, *History of the Diocese of Exeter* (Exeter, 1922), 388; *Historical Manuscripts Commission Reports* (hereafter *HMC Reports*), 9, Salisbury, XVI,

136, 443; P. Wyot, 'The Diary of Philip Wyot, 1586 – 1606', in J.R. Chanter, *Sketches of Some Striking Incidents in the History of Barnstaple* (Barnstaple, 1865), 109.

4   R. Hakluyt, *The Principall Navigations* (1589, facsimile, Cambridge, 1965), 240.

5   Public Record Office (hereafter PRO), Exchequer, King's Remembrancer Port Books, E190/935/14; Wyot, 'Diary', 96-98, 101.

6   PRO, E190 936/7; 936/6; 936/13.

7   Wyot, 'Diary', 103-4, 110.

8   *HMC Reports*, 9, Salisbury, XI, 487.

9   *Calendar of State Papers Domestic* (hereafter *CSPD*), *1601-3*, 158, 241.

10   *CSPD, 1601-3*, 292; *HMC Reports*, 9, Salisbury, 16, 6-7, 136.

11   A.L. Rowse, *The England of Elizabeth* (1964), 170; *HMC Reports*, 9, Salisbury, VIII, 252-3.

12   Wyot, 'Diary', 108; *North Devon Journal-Herald*, 7 May 1981; NDRO, NDA 98, Lease of 1608.

13   Wyot 'Diary', 113-9; NDRO, NDA 203, Lease of 1633.

14   Wyot, 'Diary', 105.

15   W. Notestein, F.H. Relf, and H. Simpson, eds, *Commons Debates 1621* (New Haven, 1935), V, 514; III, 344.

16   Notestein, *Debates 1621*, II, 364; III, 246, 373; Menna Prestwich, *Cranfield: Politics and Profits under the Early Stuarts* (Oxford, 1966), 318, 320-1, 323.

17   Notestein, *Debates 1621*, II, 249, 500; VI, 227.

18   C. Russell, *Parliaments and English Politics 1621-1629* (Oxford, 1979), 249, 341.

19   George Roberts, ed., *The Diary of Walter Yonge Esq., 1604-28* (Camden Society, 1848), 100.

20   M.F. Keeler, M.J. Cole and W.B. Bidwell, eds, *Proceedings in Parliament 1628* (New Haven and London, 1977-83), II, 314.

21 Russell, *Parliaments 1621-9*, 344.

22 Keeler, *Proceedings in Parliament 1628*, II, 227; III, 610; T.K. **Rabb**, *Enterprise and Empire* (Harvard, 1967), 233; *Calendar of State Papers Colonial* (hereafter *CSPC*); *East Indies, China and Japan, 1513-1616*, 411; *1617-21*, 506.

23 NDRO, 1142B/T10/1, 2 Deeds of 1611; PRO, Chancery Series II, 593/35, Inquisition Post Mortem, J. Delbridge.

24 A. Brown, *The Genesis of the United States* (New York, 1964), 548, 876.

25 S.M. Kingsbury, ed., *The Records of the Virginia Company of London* (Washington DC, 1906-1935), I, 259, 351, 409-10, 473; III, 309; IV, 157.

26 *HMC*, Duke of Manchester's MSS., J. Delbridge to Sir E. Sandys, 243.

27 J.H. Lefroy, *History of the Bermudas* (Hakluyt Society Publications, 1882), 188, 225, 272.

28 J.H. Lefroy, *Memorials of the Bermudas or Somers Islands, 1515-1685* (1882), I, 345, 375, 446, 448.

29 Lefroy, *Memorials of the Bermudas*, I, 443-7; *HMC Reports*, 8, Appendix, Pt. II, para. 486.

30 Lefroy, *Memorials of the Bermudas*, I, 444-8, 470-4.

31 *CSPD 1631-33*, 141, 252. *Acts of the Privy Council, Colonial Series, 1613-18*, 160.

32 PRO, E190, 947/5; J.C. Appleby, 'English Privateering in the Wars of 1625-30' (unpublished PhD thesis, University of Hull, 1983), 141.

33 Kingsbury, *Virginia Company*, IV, 157; W.R. Scott, *The Constitution and Finance of English, Scottish and Irish Joint-Stock Companies to 1720* (Cambridge, 1912), 270-80; *CSPC, North America, 1574-1669*, 48; PRO E190/945/7.

34 *CSPC, 1574-1669*, 46, 48; Kingsbury, *Virginia Company*, I, 277.

35 *CSPC, 1574-1669*, 33-4, 45-6, 157; PRO, E190 949/10, 945/7.

36 *CSPD, 1640*, 542; NDRO, NDA 3972, Receivers' Accounts f.223/2; NDRO, NDA 193 and 202, Leases of 1632-3.

37 *HMC Reports, 9*, Pt. I, 269-70; *CSPD, 1634-5*, 451; *1635*, 376; *1637*, 93; *Privy Council Registers* (facsimile, 1968), IV, f.303*v*.

38 West Country Studies Library, Will of J. Delbridge, in Olive Moger, 'Copies of Transcripts and Extracts from Wills'; *The Report of the Commissioners Concerning Charities : County of Devon* (Exeter, 1828), II, 210; C.M. Andrews, *The Colonial Period of American History* (New Haven, 1934), I, 236.

'THE SPIRIT OF PRIVATE ADVENTURE': BRITISH MERCHANTS AND THE ESTABLISHMENT OF NEW PORTS AND TRADES IN THE CAPE OF GOOD HOPE, 1795-1840[1]

E.A.G. Clark

In the early days of Dutch settlement at the Cape of Good Hope, the only port was Cape Town, where the open roadstead of Table Bay was a hazardous site for the victualling station which was the *raison d'être* for the original settlement. Even when the eastern 'colony of dispersion' began to extend far beyond the western 'colony of settlement', the Dutch continued to regard the Cape coast more as a routeway to the Indian Ocean than as a springboard for the penetration of the interior. It was only in the last years of their rule that they began to assess some of the harbours, notably Mossel Bay and Plettenberg Bay, as potential ports, instead of merely as anchorages out of the full force of the dreaded gales which threatened their East India ships.[2] This assessment had hardly got under way when the Cape was occupied by Britain in 1795. The vigour with which the assessment was continued, port sites selected, and trade fostered, suggests that the administrators of the new imperial power had a very different outlook on the role of ports and merchants in the development of overseas possessions. Their despatches were rich in empirical details, and imbued with a vigorous optimism which would have been more realistic for home waters than for a hazardous and uncharted coast six thousand miles from the English Channel.

Thus the coast of the Colony of the Cape of Good Hope is a broad canvas on which we can sketch the development of ports from the beginning. In order to focus attention on the contribution made by British merchants and seamen, the relatively short period 1795-1840 has been chosen. In these years the principal actors were from Europe, whereas the next generation of merchants was mainly native born.

The paper falls into three parts. First, the geographical setting of the ports is sketched; then the maritime activities on the Cape coast of some thirty British merchants are analysed; and, finally, the contribution they made to the development of individual ports is assessed.

The Cape of Good Hope in 1795

Table Bay Harbour was the economic pivot of the colony. In its environs half of the total population was concentrated in less than 5 per cent of the land area. Beyond the vineyards and wheat fields was the sparsely settled and semi-arid interior, given over to extensive grazing as far as the frontier district of Graaff-Reinet.[3] Scattered over this vast area were some 15000 'loan farms' of 6000 acres or more, tenuously linked with the mother city by ox waggon routes which took several weeks to traverse.[4]

The British were not sanguine at first about prospects for trade. 'We found the colony destitute of almost everything,' wrote Major-General R.S. Craig in a report on the revenue of the Cape of Good Hope.[5] Hope was expressed that 'the spirit of private adventure will induce merchants to supply the market of the Cape with every article of European produce'. The shortage of naval timber was noted, and forests surveyed at Plettenburg Bay where the Dutch had begun to trade.[6] 'To encourage vessels in every bay or other navigable port of the coast', was seen as 'the only way of giving any life to inland trade'.[7] At the beginning there was 'no shipping belonging to the colony [and] vessels are only obtainable as they happened to arrive.'[8] The Cape did not appear to possess readily exploitable resources which could become export staples, apart from wine, while the colonial market was small and handicapped by distances. Hope was expressed of introducing into England 'such a taste for the wine and raisins of the Cape, as to vanquish our preference for those of Spain, Portugal and Madeira',[9] an uphill task when Cape wine was described in the House of Commons as 'a drink only suitable for tipplers and bargemen.'[10]

Cape Town was the only established port. Although its setting was scenically magnificent, the harbour was notoriously unsafe in periods of strong NW winds, especially in winter. The Royal Navy quickly adopted the Dutch practice of using Simon's Bay instead of Table Bay between May and September, although the landing place was twenty miles from Cape Town. In 1814 all naval operations were transferred to Simon's Bay.[11] Cape Town had formerly been a refreshment station on the way to the Dutch East Indies. The British wanted to extend the 'half way house' functions for it to 'become the centre of commerce with India, America and Europe.'[12] 1095 vessels called at the port between 1795 and 1803, including 271 British East Indiamen, 302 other British vessels, 215 American, and 134 Danish.[13] The East India Company's monopoly of trade with all ports east of the Cape of Good Hope was proclaimed, and opportunities for independent commercial enterprise by English merchants were restricted to the coasting trade and the Atlantic.[14] Several British merchants established themselves in Cape Town and traded in the Indian Ocean on behalf of the Company.[15] Our concern, however, is with those merchants who looked beyond Cape Town and founded new ports on the Cape coast to develop the interior of the colony.

Each of us tends to see the world in a slightly different way because of differences in experience, values and interests. Mariners brought assumptions from England about the importance of the coasting trade and the value of 'tide havens' and sheltered anchorages. They computed depths on river bars and investigated anchorages for shelter from prevailing winds. In contrast, merchants tended to see the coast in terms of possible cargoes and hinterlands, and often lacked a discerning eye for the potential of harbours. Ports are complicated entities to perceive,

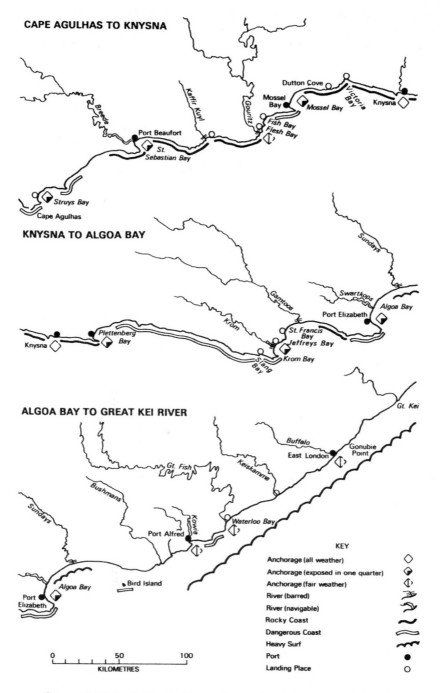

CAPE AGULHAS TO KNYSNA

Dutton Cove
Mossel Bay
Mossel Bay
Victoria Bay
Knysna
Kaffir Kuyl
Gouritz
Fish Bay
Flesh Bay
Breede
Port Beaufort
St. Sebastian Bay
Struys Bay
Cape Agulhas

KNYSNA TO ALGOA BAY

Sundays
Swartkops
Algoa Bay
Port Elizabeth
Garntoos
Krom
St. Francis Bay
Jeffreys Bay
Plettenberg Bay
Knysna
Slang Bay
Krom Bay

ALGOA BAY TO GREAT KEI RIVER

Gt. Kei
Buffalo
Gonubie Point
East London
Gt. Fish
Keiskamma
Bushmans
Sundays
Waterloo Bay
Kowie
Port Alfred
Bird Island
Algoa Bay
Port Elizabeth

KEY

Anchorage (all weather)	◇
Anchorage (exposed in one quarter)	◈
Anchorage (fair weather)	⬨
River (barred)	⤳
River (navigable)	⤳
Rocky Coast	∼
Dangerous Coast	≈
Heavy Surf	⌇
Port	●
Landing Place	○

0   50   100
KILOMETRES

Source: EAG Clark, *South African Geographical Journal* (1977), p. 152.

involving such problems as the evaluation of hazards and the gauging of hinterlands. Weather, sea and submarine channel conditions varied from day to day. The immigrant merchants made decisions on the basis of frames of reference brought from northern seas. Results in the form of delays and disappointments, or satisfactory profits and burgeoning trade, provided feedback and the evaluation continued.[16]

In 1795 there was fairly detailed cartographical knowledge of the bays and promontories of the Cape, but no accurate surveys had been made of individual harbours and tidal rivers. In 1798 Lt. Rice was sent in the brig *Hope* 'to explore ... the almost totally unknown coast of Africa east of the Cape'. Rice was joined by John Barrow, who was on a tour of scientific research.[17] In his books Barrow published maps and descriptions of the Cape coast which were the most detailed in print until the first Admiralty *Pilot* in 1856.[18] In 1820 Captain Moresby was commissioned to report on the coast of the Eastern Cape and about this time detailed surveys were made of the Kowie and the Great Fish rivers.[19] Nevertheless, opinion was still divided about the merits of the numerous landing places and rivers.

The coast east of Cape Town can be divided into two contrasting sections.[20] The western one is dominated by ten wide embayments, each with a sheltered anchorage on the western side, out of the winter storms but exposed to the summer easterlies. Five of these bays became the sites of ports in our period: False (Simon's Town), St. Sebastian's (Port Beaufort), Mossel, Plettenberg, and Algoa (Port Elizabeth). St. Sebastian's Bay has a navigable river, the Breede, entered through an intricate channel with 7 feet at low water. The other navigable river is at Knysna, where a large lagoon provides a deep natural harbour with a narrow cliff-fringed entrance with 13 feet of water on the bar.

East of Algoa Bay the coast is straighter and there are fewer stretches of cliff. Most of the rivers were barred, and the remainder have intricate and shallow entrances. There were many attempts to develop river ports but only at the Kowie (Port Alfred) and the Buffalo (East London) was there any success. Even in these cases the depth on the bars fluctuated between 2 and 7 feet until the river mouths were deepened as part of costly harbour schemes in the second half of the nineteenth century.[21]

Heavy surf was a hazard on this section of coast, and the lack of sheltered anchorages increased the vulnerability of shipping in the days of sail. An Admiralty chart recorded: 'the severity of the gales off the Cape of Good Hope and the adjacent coast to the eastward is well known to navigators, as also the rapidity with which they succeed one another and their violence during the winter months'.[22]

The English merchants soon learned that conditions were very different from home waters. Only the rivers Breede, Knysna, Kowie and Buffalo offered possibilities for the development of sheltered river ports, and the intricacies of the entrance channels made approach hazardous in poor weather. A typical sloop or schooner of the early nineteenth century drew 9 feet of water, brigs of 100 to 200 tons 10 to 14 feet, while the large East Indiamen drew 21 feet.[23] Apart from the Knysna no river ports in the Cape of Good Hope had more than 7 feet on the bar at low water, and thus even with a tidal rise of 5 feet they were closed to larger vessels, especially when the safety margin and the effects of pitching and rolling are taken into account. At Port Alfred, for example, it was found necessary to provide special shallow-draft lighters to unload vessels lying outside the bar, and to initiate a coasting service with small schooners of 25 tons burthen.[24] The small size of cargoes available at the embryonic coastal ports also influenced the trend to use small schooners. In 1829 most of the coasting trade was carried by nine 'regular traders' (mainly schooners and cutters), each making three or four voyages each way between Cape Town and Algoa Bay (Port Elizabeth).[25]

The Merchants

Because of the considerable historical and genealogical interest in British emigration to the Cape, especially that of the 1820 settlers, a rich store of biographical detail is available. Virtually all of those merchants shown in the records as engaging in maritime trade in the Cape before 1825 can be identified in Peter Philip's list of *British Residents at the Cape 1795-1819* (1981), or in E. Morse Jones' *Roll of the British Settlers* (1971). Even after 1825 most of the merchants can be traced. The record of sailings to and from ports is fairly comprehensive, albeit scattered, but that of merchants' consignments is patchy and scattered through the Cape archives.[26] Details of ship ownership in our period are sometimes hard to find. Cumulatively, then, a fairly comprehensive picture can be built up of the movement of coastwise shipping and the part played by individual merchants. The merchants active in maritime trade along the coast of the Cape of Good Hope can be divided into six groups according to their previous experience.

(i)   Merchants already experienced in maritime trade, who came to the Cape to open a new theatre of operations.

Most of these immigrants had sufficient capital and experience to embark in trade soon after their arrival.

Henry Nourse (1781-1834) was a London merchant and shipowner who began trading with the Cape in 1806. His first agent, Kenneth Duncan of Edinburgh, married in 1809 the daughter of Konstent Ondruydt, President of the Burgher Senate of Cape Town and owner of vessels engaged in the coasting trade. From 1813 Nourse's affairs at the Cape were managed by his brother-in-law, Ewan Christian, a Mauritius merchant who moved to Cape Town. In 1818 Nourse proposed an emigration scheme to the government. For an investment of twenty pounds per head, indentured labourers from England could be contracted out at a return of thirty to one hundred pounds a head. He added, 'I am sensible that objections may be taken to the plan I suggest on the idea of its being a species of slavery'. He then came out to the Cape, bringing, in Lord Charles Somerset's words, 'strong and particular letters and documents on his behalf from the Secretary of State's office ... which made it imperative on me to show him every practicable attention to his commercial plans ... to form seven different commercial establishments in different parts of the colony'. Somerset granted him nearly four thousand acres near Port Alfred. Nourse appointed agents at Port Elizabeth and Bathurst, and claimed that he had 'at least thirty if not forty thousand rix dollars capital floating between my two establishments'. His scheme hinged on the supply of salt beef and other provisions from Algoa Bay for the navy. He was helped by the appointment of his brother Joseph to be commodore of the Cape naval station. He invited him to see 'the superiority of the pasturage and the appearance of the cattle' on his Bathurst farm. He had four vessels in the coasting trade, the *Jane, Elizabeth, Mary,* and *Orange Grove.* The last-named made three voyages each way between Cape Town and Port Elizabeth in 1829, while the *Elizabeth,* with 25 tons of cargo for Nourse, was, in 1821, the first vessel to use the Kowie. In 1823 Captain Joseph Nourse surveyed the Kowie and recommended the dredging and straightening of the river. When the customs establishment was withdrawn in 1826, Henry Nourse purchased the customs house. He was now based in Grahamstown, exporting wool from Port Elizabeth, purchasing land on the border, and acting as an agent for the so-called 'Kaffir trade' beyond the border.[27]

John Murray (1749-1815) was a merchant from Aberdeen who arrived in the Cape in 1797. The following year he purchased a whale fishery belonging to Messrs. Fehrson, operating in Mossel, Plettenberg and Algoa Bays. Murray also purchased a coasting vessel, the *Alert,* and plied between Cape Town and Mossel Bay, taking haberdashery, clothes, glass and iron ware to trade with the farmers, and returning with timber from the Outeniquas. He had a farm at Mossel Bay with six slaves and 52 trek oxen.[28]

A contrast to Murray's rustic idyll is offered by the career of William Wilberforce Bird, member of a prominent silk and manufacturing family of Coventry, who emigrated to the Cape in 1807. He took out a licence for a French prize he named the *Betsy.* He also had shares in four other vessels. Until he became controller of customs for the colony in 1811 he was one of its most prominent merchants, trading to St. Helena, Mauritius and Reunion.[29]

Francis Farewell (1793-1829), the son of a Somerset rector, served in the navy, then went to India to trade as a shipowner. Farewell arrived in Cape Town in 1818, and began to enlist support for a scheme to develop the ivory trade on the little known coast of Natal. Making use of recent naval surveys, he sailed to Port Natal and St. Lucia. He then persuaded the Cape governor to authorise a trading venture in Natal, and sailed with thirty supporters to negotiate an agreement with the Zulu king, Chaka. His unpublished correspondence is rich in details of the organisation of the ivory trade, and the backing he received from London merchants. He was murdered in 1829 while on an overland journey to Natal.[30]

Michael Hogan, an Irish merchant, arrived in Cape Town in 1798, and was given special permission to import timber and rice from Bengal. Between 1799 and

1801 he became the owner of a coasting vessel, *La Rose*, and some ten other vessels, mainly fitted with guns and issued with letters of marque. With Alexander Tennant, a Scot, he engaged in slave trading on the Mocambique and West African coasts. They used privateers for an elaborate subterfuge to import slaves illegally, by pretending that the ships transporting slaves had been captured as prizes. At a court hearing evidence was led that 'the two supposed prizes were not captured, as has long been stated, but were purchased at Mozambique'.[31]

Other Cape Town merchants were implicated in this illicit trade. To the embarrassment of Sir George Yonge, Governor of the Cape, one of the ships belonging to Walker and Robertson, the *Lady Yonge*, bore his wife's name. The case revealed the 'very improper engagements' entered into by the governor. Lady Anne Barnard wrote in her diary that the governor was to leave Government House and reside with Walker and Robertson, 'merchants to save whom he has made so many stretches of power'. Yonge gave them a timber monopoly at Plettenberg Bay. Their coasting vessel was the *Young Nicholas*. Alexander Walker and John Robertson were both from Scotland. They began business in the East Indian trade and in 1800 became the first licensed printers of the colony, publishing a weekly newspaper. Another vessel of theirs, the *Chesterfield*, was apprehended in the contraband trade on the South American coast.[32]

(ii) Merchants who began their career in the Cape in a subordinate position in a mercantile house, and later opened on their own account.

This small group includes three of the most successful and influential merchants of their era. By definition they were self-made men, but their contribution to the public life of their communities was notable.

John Bardwell Ebden was the son of an army surgeon. Of adventurous disposition, he embarked on a voyage to China at the age of sixteen, and was shipwrecked at the Cape on his return. He worked as a clerk in naval victualling, then two years later, in 1808, set up in partnership with Robert Watts, another clerk. They traded on licence with goods from India, and also sent cargoes to St. Helena. By 1814 they had a brig, the *Brissett*, in this trade. Ebden was a founder of the Cape of Good Hope Trade Society in 1825, and in the same year founded the first bank in the Cape. Like other prominent Cape Town merchants, he was interested in the frontier trade in the 1830s, and also took the lead in the establishment of the Steam Navigation Company in 1836. Significantly, he did not venture much capital in the risky coasting trade. Later he became a prominent colonial politician.[33]

Joseph Barry (1796-1865) was born in Hertfordshire and trained for the wine trade in France and Spain, before coming to Cape Town in 1817 as agent for a wine firm. Through contacts with Henry Nourse he began to speculate in part cargoes to coastal ports. In 1822 he chartered a cutter, the *Duke of Gloucester*, to carry rice and barley to Port Beaufort to supply the Swellendam district, then suffering from drought. He developed a coasting trade serving the rich farmlands of the Overberg region, and built warehouses at Port Beaufort, Swellendam and Mossel Bay. Shipments included grain, horns, skins and wool. Barry owned farms and pioneered the rearing of merino sheep. His firm, Barry and Nephews, had branches and shops in many of the small towns of the south-western Cape, with the managers characteristically members of his extended family. Barry married Johanna van Reenen, a member of a leading Dutch family, and this connection was, in his own words, 'the secret of his success'. In 1803 D.G. van Reenen had pointed out the potential of the harbour on the Breede River, and Port Beaufort became the pivot of Barry's commercial empire. He held the majority of shares in the Port Beaufort Trading Company, formed in 1820 in association with the Cape Town merchants Ewan Christian and Francis Collison. To begin with he hired vessels, for example, the *Kowie Packet*, to fulfil a government victualling contract he undertook at Port Frances (later Port Alfred). Later he owned two brigs, the *Singapore* and the *Fanny*, and the schooners *Good Intent* and *Barrys*. In 1859 he purchased the *Kadie* steamer to open up the Breede River port of Malagas 15 miles upstream. The *Kadie* made some twenty voyages a year to Cape Town.[34]

John Owen Smith (1804-1871) came from Scarborough where his family were ship owners. When still a youth he joined his uncle, a ship's captain, in Cape Town. After spending some time in Grahamstown he established himself in Port Elizabeth in 1830 as a shipping agent. He began trading with Port Natal and supplied arms to the Boer trekkers there. Smith's vessel, the *Mazeppa*, rescued survivors of Louis Trichardt's party in Lourenco Marques and took them to Port Natal. The *Mazeppa* explored the coast between the Buffalo (later the site of East London) and Port Natal to find a suitable landing place for a trading station he established in Transkeian territories. From 1840 Smith operated one of the three boating establishments at Port Elizabeth, unloading ships in Algoa Bay. In 1844 he constructed a jetty and a private railway to expedite port operations. He owned farms in the Eastern Cape, had a vessel engaged in the guano trade in the Bird Island, and in 1853 fitted out the *Emily Smith* to transport copper ore from Namaqualand, where he leased mining rights, making use of the port of Alexander Bay.[35]

(iii) Merchants who began as landowners in the Cape of Good Hope, and turned to maritime trade to market their farming produce.

This was also a small but influential group of merchants, active in the early days of British occupation in the Cape. Their existence is indicative of the undeveloped business structure of the Cape at this time.

Benjamin Moodie (1789-1856) was the eldest son of the laird of Melsetter in Orkney. In 1817 he contracted with a Cape Town merchant, Hamilton Ross, for the large-scale emigration of Scottish settlers to the Cape. He purchased a farm in the

Overberg grainlands and, like Joseph Barry, used Port Beaufort, where he established a warehouse paid for by subscription shares. In contrast to Barry, who sold on commission, he took the risk of purchasing farm products in the Overberg and selling them in the Cape Town market. In 1828 he joined Barry in the Port Beaufort Trading Company. In later life his interests included farming, philanthropy (for example, the Children's Friend Society which sent vagrant children as emigrants to the Cape), and he held a seat in the Cape Assembly.[36]

The maritime interests of Moodie's brother, Donald, are described below.

George Rex (1765-1839) was the son of a prosperous Whitechapel brewer. Rumours which still persist said that he was the eldest son of George III by a morganatic union with the Quaker, Hannah Lightfoot. Rex came to the Cape in 1795 and was appointed notary public. On the reversion of the Cape to the Batavian Republic in 1803 he turned to farming and purchased a farm on Knysna lagoon. Eventually he owned 35,000 acres in the region. He encouraged the Royal Navy to develop the rich timber resources, making use of his contacts made when he was Marshal of the Vice Admiralty Court. In 1811 he took out a licence to employ 400 wood cutters at Plettenberg Bay. For more than a decade some 5-10 shipments of timber were sent annually to Cape Town. A surviving business ledger shows Rex's transactions with ships' captains, and the variety of goods for the neighbourhood traded at his storehouse on the bay. His ship, the *Young Phoenix*, made four voyages to Cape Town in some years. Rex exported butter to Port Elizabeth, St. Helena and Mauritius. The lagoon port of Knysna was opened in 1818, and there were eight shipments of timber the following year. In 1836 Rex's son, John, tendered his brig, the *Knysna*, to transport government stores from Cape Town to a new landing place near the frontier, to serve the military in British Kaffraria. The vessel was too large to enter the Buffalo River, but discharged in the mouth. The new port, later East London, was called Port Rex.[37]

A major change in the economic centre of gravity in the Cape occurred with the arrival of the 1820 English settlers. In a large government-assisted scheme 4,000 emigrants were landed at Port Elizabeth, and located in agricultural settlements between the port and the Great Fish River frontier. The search for a more central port for this settlement engaged much attention.

John Bailie (1788-1852), son of a subaltern in the East India Company army, was leader of a large party of settlers located near the River Kowie. He surveyed the river and took part in the deliberations which led to the establishment of Port Frances and also of the Kowie River Navigation Company. In 1822 he surveyed the neighbouring coast, and advocated the establishment of a port at the mouth of the Great Fish River, near his farm 'The Hope'. In 1836 Bailie was instructed by the military authorities to survey the mouth of the Buffalo river, which he suggested as a landing place for military supplies. He sailed from Knysna in George Rex's ship of that name, disembarked at Port Elizabeth and rode overland to the Buffalo to superintend the entry of the *Knysna*. Today a plaque erroneously records his hoisting of the Union Jack on Signal Hill overlooking East London. Between 1839 and 1844 Bailie was secretary of the Port Elizabeth Jetty Company. He then left the Cape to join his son in the Caledon district, north of the Orange River, and was sentenced to death following a quarrel which culminated in Bailie killing the commandant of the Boers in that district. Eventually he was granted a free pardon, and was appointed supervisor of the newly formed Natal Cotton Company (of which J.B. Ebden was chairman). The company failed and Bailie set himself up as an agent to R.P. (Dick) King. Bailie then fitted out the *Haidee* for a trading voyage to the Umtata River. A newspaper report referred to Bailie's 'intimate topographical knowledge of the coast to the south of Durban', and his intention to judge 'the openings for commerce and colonisation'. Bailie sold his provisions, soap, 'kafir' picks and other merchandise, and purchased gum, but was drowned attempting to assist the crew of a vessel which had foundered.[38]

William Cock (1793-1876) from Penryn, Cornwall, also came to the Cape in 1820 as the head of a party of settlers. His land was near the Kowie river and he soon abandoned farming for commerce. He traded commodities for stock and provisions which he sold in Grahamstown, Port Elizabeth and Cape Town. In 1826 he purchased a vessel to transport salt beef and butter to St. Helena from Algoa Bay. Later he opened markets in Mauritius and Port Natal, and in 1835 supplied provisions to the troops in the Sixth Frontier War. He was one of the first merchants to export merino wool from Port Elizabeth.[39]

In 1839 Cock succeeded in getting a Private Bill passed for 'the opening and improvement of the River Kowie', by Heideman, Cock and Company. The scheme was to make a straight cut for the river through the sandbanks. Two entrance piers, 120 feet apart, defined the new entrance. The *Nautical Magazine* published sailing directions for the reconstructed port, and it was hoped that vessels drawing 10-12 feet would be able to enter. Cock floated the Kowie Harbour Improvement Company in 1842, and the Kowie Navigation Company in 1843. He purchased a paddle steamer of 175 tons, the *Sir John Aubyn*, which accomplished the voyage from Cape Town in four days, but sank in the Kowie in 1843. Vessels coming to Port Alfred continued to run aground, and the new harbour works were damaged by floods. Cock refused to give up. His vessels the *British Settler* and the *Chanticleer* continued to use the Kowie, until the former was wrecked. In 1847 Cock was nominated for the Cape Legislative Council and he immediately pressed for a commission to examine the navigational potential of the Kowie. The Kowie Harbour Improvement Company was formed in 1853. The plan was for a mile of embankments to confine the river to a uniformly wide channel, entered between long piers. These ambitious works dragged on for years. The company was dissolved in 1876 and the scheme taken over by the government. It was not completed until 1889. Meanwhile William Cock had died in 1876.[40]

(iv) Merchants who came to the Cape originally as seafarers.

Some seventy British vessels were calling at Cape Town annually in 1795-1803. Some of the ships' masters were regular visitors and they began to take an interest in commercial speculation at the Cape.

Thomas Melville (1757-1841) was master of a whaler fishing in Pacific waters. He settled in the Cape in 1799, purchased a small schooner and embarked for Saldanha Bay north of Cape Town where he bought a share in a farm. By 1807 he was in business with Joseph Johnson as ship chandlers and owned the brigs *Fanny* and *Discovery*, which traded to Plettenberg Bay for timber.[41]

Christopher Mackoy, master mariner, was appointed harbour master at Port Frances in 1822. He sent beef to Cape Town on the *Frances*, and in 1826 purchased the *Buck Bay Packet*, with several prominent Albany settlers, including Bailie, standing surety for him. In 1828 he sailed to Port Natal to trade for ivory. He went on to the Maputu river where the *Buck Bay Packet* was wrecked and Mackoy died of fever.[42]

Donald Moodie (1796-1861) was a lieutenant in the Royal Navy and a brother of Benjamin Moodie. He visited the Cape on his way to India in 1820, and joined Benjamin on a farm east of Algoa Bay. The following year he made observations on the possible navigation of the Kowie. He married the daughter of a prominent Albany settler, Major George Pigot, and was appointed magistrate at Port Frances. Donald took the initiative in establishing the Albany Shipping Company and there were plans for purchasing two or three small schooners to navigate the shallow estuary. Moodie grasped the point that the Kowie was too shallow for large coasters, and advocated the use of a steam dredger in the entrance. Later Moodie moved to Natal, where he was Colonial Secretary in 1845, and Speaker of the Legislative Council in 1857.[43]

John Biddulph (1796-1837), was a member of Bailie's party of settlers. He had served in the Royal Navy as a midshipman, without obtaining a commission. He made a survey and map of the Kowie river in 1820. Biddulph had a farm and made profitable overland trading expeditions beyond the colonial frontier, including three expeditions to Natal. Eventually he moved to Graaff Reinet as a farmer and commission agent.[44]

Edward Wallace (1791-1832) was a master mariner from London, engaged in the St. Helena trade. In 1820 he became pilot at Knysna, then successively harbour master of Port Frances and Port Elizabeth. Thus he contributed to the development of three of the new Cape ports.[45]

James Callander (1758-1820) was a master mariner from Scotland. Soon after his arrival in the Cape he was authorised by the government to examine the forests, bays and rivers of the Knysna region. He reported that the river was deep enough for small vessels of 10 feet draught, and recommended the exploitation of the neighbouring forests for the navy. He returned to the sea as master of vessels in the Cape trade, then became a merchant in Cape Town.[46]

James Saunders King (1795-1828) came to the Cape in 1820 after service in the navy. In 1822 he commanded the *Salisbury* plying between Cape Town and Algoa Bay. The following year the vessel was fitted out by F.G. Farewell and J.R. Thompson to explore trading prospects beyond the eastern frontier. The *Salisbury* was forced into Port Natal in a gale and King made a detailed map of the harbour. Two years later he returned in the *Mary* but the vessel was wrecked entering Port Natal. King salvaged the cargo and traded with the Zulus, but died of dysentery.

Several other master mariners entered the coasting trade, including R. Kelly of the *Albert*, W.T. Morse of the *Louisa*, Henry Phillips of the *Friends*, and Henry Steward.[48]

(v) **Merchants who came to the Eastern Cape in the wake of the 1820 Settlement Scheme.**

This group included many of the merchants who contributed to the rise of Port Elizabeth as a major commercial centre. Henry Maynard, for example, acted as agent for Nourse in Delagoa Bay in 1823. In 1826 he and his brother Charles were exporting tallow, skins and hides from Port Frances. Charles was on the committee of the Port Elizabeth Jetty Company. By 1832 the brothers were shipping agents in Port Elizabeth and Grahamstown, advertising a range of haberdashery, kitchen and iron ware imported from London. Later the firm of Maynard and Wood owned the schooner *Seaforth*. An interest was maintained in both local ports and Charles was Chairman of the Port Frances Harbour Commission in 1850.[49]

Other merchants trading on a small scale from Port Frances in the 1820s included Henry Henderson, John Maskell and Alexander Kidwell.[50] An example of enterprise is provided by Thomas Oldham of Bailie's party, a tanner by trade. He purchased a wreck on the coast and built a small schooner, the *Perseverance*, which he operated on the coast in partnership with his brother, who lived in Cape Town, and James Scott, a merchant of Port Elizabeth.[51]

(vi) **Dutch merchants and merchants from the continent of Europe.**

The small part played by Dutch inhabitants of the Cape in the early coasting trade is striking. In 1801 four coasting vessels were Dutch-owned, including two belonging to Frederick Korsten (sometimes 'Kirsten' or 'Kersten'). Korsten (1773-1839) served in the Dutch navy, then settled in Cape Town where he married the daughter of a Dutch merchant. In 1812, together with Carel Pohl and Roger Metelerkamp, he contracted to deliver 2,000 barrels of salted beef to British forces at Algoa Bay. He built a salting plant, mill and tannery at his farm there, and had a whale fishery in the bay. Korsten owned three coasting vessels, the *Uitenhage Packet*, the *Thomas* and the *Winifred and Maria*, and is often regarded as the founder of Port Elizabeth's trade.[52]

Another Dutch merchant engaged in the coasting trade was W. Liesching, who shipped corn from Lambert's Bay to Cape Town.[53]

Anthony Chiappini was born in Italy in 1776 but brought up in England. He emigrated to the Cape in 1805 and became a leading merchant and chairman of the Commercial Exchange. He owned a coasting schooner, the *Flamingo*, which plied between Cape Town and Algoa Bay and Port Frances, and other vessels which carried grain from Algoa Bay to Mauritius.[54]

Conclusion

The thirty English merchants whose commercial enterprises we have outlined made two major contributions to the economic life of the Cape. In the first place, they established a regular coasting trade, linking some twelve harbours between Saldanha Bay, north-west of Cape Town, and Port Natal, beyond the eastern frontier of Cape Colony. Between them they owned at least twenty-three coasting vessels. Until 1820 the coasting trade was intermittent. Most English merchants left the Cape when it reverted to the Batavian Republic between 1803 and 1806, and trade was slow to revive. The colonial government found it necessary to provide suitable vessels for coastal service, including the *Isabella, Agnes, Buck Bay Packet* and *Frances*. Sir Rufane Donkin had plans for increasing the coasting trade, and for establishing a port on the south eastern coast. Coastwise shipments to Cape Town (excluding short hauls) increased from 6-10 annually in 1807-9, to 19-22 in 1818-20.[55]

After 1820 trade expanded rapidly. The Albany settlers formed a substantial market near the frontier, more than 500 miles from Cape Town. Grain, hides, tallow and wool were return cargoes. Cape Town was the pivot, with 30 inward shipments in 1825. The *Usk, George IV, George*, and *Flamingo* each made two voyages to Algoa Bay, while the *Kowie Packet* and *Elizabeth* plied to Port Frances. On the shorter hauls in the western Cape, Barry's *Good Intent* made six voyages to Port Beaufort, the *Saldhana Bay Packet* five, and the *Buck Bay Packet* seven voyages. By 1829 there were nine regular coasting vessels on the Algoa Bay route, each making three or four voyages annually, with occasional intermediate calls at Mossel Bay and Port Beaufort. A coasting trade had been established, linking the western and eastern parts of Cape Colony.[56]

The second major achievement of the English merchants was the establishment of six new ports: Port Beaufort, Knysna, Port Elizabeth, Port Frances (later Port Alfred), Port Rex (later East London), and Port Natal (later Durban).

In 1800 Sir George Yonge called for a report on the suitability of the Breede river for shipping. It was said to be navigable for 'up to six hours inland'. Three years later D.G. van Reenen, Joseph Barry's father-in-law, advised, 'at the side of the mouth is a good anchorage, and it would be possible to ship the products grown in these parts in small vessels'. The first recorded shipment was of corn to Cape Town in 1816. The following year Lord Charles Somerset ordered a survey, and named the harbour Port Beaufort. Moodie and Barry built warehouses, and later joined with Nourse, Christian and Collison in the Fort Beaufort Trading Company. Nine vessels discharged in 1824.

At first George Rex used Mossel and Plettenberg Bays for timber shipments from the Outenique forests. In 1817 shipments began from the Knysna, which James Callander had described in 1799 as 'the best situation on this coast for shipping timber, having a small island immediately within the narrow entrance, where fifty shiploads of timber may lay'. Five vessels discharged in 1824 and a customs officer was stationed at the port.[58]

In Algoa Bay the landing place near the mouth of the Baakens river was used from 1799 by vessels supplying Fort Frederick. The earliest commercial shipments were of salted beef to Cape Town and Mauritius by Korsten and Nourse, from 1813. Algoa Bay was the port for the 1820 settlement, and the number of ships discharging there rose from 6 in 1820 to 50 in 1830. Hides, skins and merino wool were the chief exports. Nourse, Smith, Cock, Korsten, Chiappini and Maynard played major parts in the expansion of trade at Port Elizabeth, which was hailed as 'the Liverpool of the Cape'.[59]

The River Kowie was closer to the Albany settlement than was Algoa Bay. Many pinned their hopes on developing a river port inside the shallow entrance. Bailie, Moodie, Biddulph and Joseph Nourse all made surveys. Henry Nourse and Donald Moodie accompanied the governor, Sir Rufane Donkin, on an investigation in 1821. Donkin reported, 'I am making all necessary arrangements [for] a trade between Bathurst and Cape Town, by way of the Kowie'. His successor, Lord Charles Somerset, authorised the construction of a customs house. Nourse's vessel, the *Elizabeth* was the first to enter.[60] When the *Elizabeth* was wrecked in 1822 Somerset authorised the construction of two schooners to act as lighters for vessels on the bar. The recommended procedure was to leave the laden vessels lying on the sand until full tide, and then draw them through the channel with ropes. By 1826 it was reported that 'the difficulty attending the entrance of the River Kowie ... have deterred almost all the traders from frequenting Port Francis.' An official enquiry concluded: 'I have no hesitation in strongly recommending that it be entirely done away with, as I am fully convinced ... that it can never be a place of resort for shipping.[61] The attempts made by William Cock to reopen the port in 1839 have already been described.

East of the Kowie the Fish River formed the frontier of settlement, and the coasting trade was in an embryonic stage until Natal was taken under British sovereignty in 1844. In 1836 Bailie advocated the development of the Buffalo mouth as a harbour for the new province of Queen Adelaide. John Rex's *Knysna* brought military supplies and loaded hides and horns obtained through barter with the Xhosa. He advertised the new port in the *Graham's Town Journal* but no further trade took place following the abandonment of the new province. In 1847 the Buffalo was used again for the discharge of military supplies. Fort Glamorgan was built, and in the following year the settlement was proclaimed the port of East London.[62]

Farewell was the first merchant to visit the little known harbour of Port Natal for trading purposes. In 1823 his associate, James Saunders King, made a detailed map of the harbour. Within the next decades Mackoy, Nourse, Biddulph, Cock, Smith, Maynard, and Bailie traded to Port Natal or the neighbouring coast.

* * * * * * *

At the beginning of the first British occupation of the Cape, General Craig had looked to 'the spirit of private adventure' to solve the problems posed by its undeveloped business structure. The thirty merchants we have considered rose to the challenge of meagre and uncertain markets, distance, threatening seas, and unpredictable harbours. Each formed his own perception of commercial opportunities, and provided a model of mercantile enterprise for their contemporaries to emulate or avoid. Varied in their backgrounds, personalities and degrees of success, they exhibit a sample of that pioneer enterprise which cumulatively led to the development of a more mature commercial system in the next generation.

Among the most successful were entrepreneurs like Nourse, Smith and Chiappini, whose business interests were widely spread in the colony, and Barry, Rex, Cock and Korsten, who concentrated their efforts in one region or port, where their commercial acumen remains a legend today. Another group of successful merchants gave up trading to dedicate their talents to public service, including Bird, Ebden and the two Moodies. Then there were those adventurers who operated beyond the normal frontier of commerce, such as Farewell, Bailie, King and Mackoy, all of whom met their deaths while attempting to open sea links with Natal. Finally, there were the less colourful, less conspicuously successful merchants of whom relatively little is known. Although they did not make large fortunes from maritime trade, together their contribution to the establishment of new ports and sea-borne commerce in the Cape was also considerable.

NOTES

1   An early version of this paper was read at the Dartington Conference in October 1983. I am grateful for comments made on that occasion.

2   For the Dutch assessment see George M. Theal, *Belangrike Historische Dokumenten over Zuid Afrika* (Cape Town, De Schadt de Villiers, 1911), III, 36-9; S. Daniel Neumark, *Economic Influences on the South African Frontier, 1652-1836* (Stanford University Press, 1957), 61-2, 137-140; A.L. Muller, 'Coastal shipping and the early development of the Southern Cape', *Contree*, 18 (1985), 10-15.

3   Neumark, *Economic Influences*, 27-40, 70-93; Anthony J. Christopher, *Southern Africa* (Folkestone, Dawson, 1976), 29-54.

4   George M. Theal, *Records of the Cape Colony 1793-1831* (London, Clowes, 1897-1905), I, 254, 264.

5   Theal, *Records*, I, 284.

6   Theal, *Records*, II, 281; III, 379.

7   Theal, *Records*, X, 89.

8   Theal, *Records*, III, 504.

9   Theal, *Records*, II, 117.

10 Marcus Arkin, 'John Company at the Cape', *Archives Yearbook for South African History*, 23 (1961), 2, 248-9.

11 Theal, *Records*, II, 254; IV, 58, 78; William W. Bird, *State of the Cape of Good Hope in 1822* (London, John Murray, 1823).

12 Theal, *Records*, III.

13 Arkin, 'John Company', 201.

14 For details of controls, see British Parliamentary Papers, *Report of the Commissioners of Inquiry upon the Trade of the Cape of Good Hope* (1829), V(300), 3-12.

15 Ebden and Watts; Hamilton Ross; Short and Berry; William Robertson; Hall and Rowe; Arkin, 'John Company', *passim*.

16 Edwin A.G. Clark, 'Port Sites and Perception: the Development of the Southern and Eastern Cape Coast in the Nineteenth Century', *South African Geographical Journal*, LIX(2) (1977), 150-67.

17 Theal, *Records*, II, 88.

18 John Barrow, *Accounts of Travels into the Interior of South Africa* (London, Cadell and Davies, 1801, 1804).

19 Theal, *Records*, XIII, 185-93; XIV, 235.

20 Great Britain, Admiralty, *Africa, South and East Coasts* (London, 1861); Great Britain, Admiralty, *African Pilot*, Vol. III (London, HMSO, 1967); United States Navy, *Sailing Directions for the South-east Coast of Africa* (New York, 1936).

21 Clark, 'Port Sites', 159-60.

22 Great Britain, Admiralty, *Cape of Good Hope from Hondeklip Bay to Durban* (chart) (London, 1867).

23 D. Steel, *The Elements and Practice of Naval Architecture* (London, 1822); Edwin A.G. Clark, *The Ports of the Exe Estuary, 1660-1860* (Exeter, University of Exeter Press, 1960), 16.

24 See pp. 124-5.

25 Analysed in *Cape Town Gazette and African Advertiser*, fortnightly edition, 1829.

26 Records of ship movements with dates are summarised in, *African Court Calendar*, annually, 1801-17; *Cape Almanac*, 1818-40. They can be traced, with more difficulty, in the fortnightly 'Shipping Intelligence' notices in *Cape Town Gazette and African Advertizer*. There are also records of ship movements in Cape Town, Government Archives, Colonial Office, Letters Received, Several Bays, 1821-1841; C.O.6099, Reports of arrival of ships, 1820-1826 (include Port Frances, Algoa Bay, Plettenburg Bay, Knysna, Mossel Bay and Port Beaufort); P.O. 3/1, Registers of arrivals and departures of ships, Table Bay, 1806-40.

27 Peter Philip, *British Residents at the Cape, 1795-1819* (Cape Town, David Philip, 1981), 306; *Dictionary of South African Biography* (*DSAB*) (Petoria, HSRC, 1968 etc.) III, 600. Theal, *Records*, XI, 446-8; XV, 79, 103; XVII, 31-3; Johannesburg, University of the Witwatersrand Library, Nourse Family Papers; Basil A. Le Cordeur, *The Politics of Eastern Cape Separatism* (Cape

Town, OUP, 1981), 40, 54, 72, 89; E. Morse Jones, *LAC* (*Lower Albany Chronicle*, Lower Albany Historical Society, Port Alfred, South Africa), 1802-25 (1968), II, 1826-40 (1964).

28 Philip, *British Residents*, 297-8; Muller, 'Coastal Shipping', 10-15; Henry H.C. Lichtenstein, *Travels in Southern Africa in the Years 1802, 1804, 1805 and 1806* (London, Colburn, 1812).

29 Philip, *British Residents*, 28; *DSAB*, I, 77-9; Arkin, *passim*.

30 Philip, *British Residents*, 123; *DSAB*, I, 286-7; (London, PRO, C.O. 148, 135, Correspondence of Lt. Farewell); Theal, *Records*, XVII, 231-2; XVIII, 122-4.

31 Theal, *Records*, II, 315, 378; IV, 262-73; Philip, *British Residents*, 182-3.

32 Philip, *British Residents*, 349-50, 442.

33 Philip, *British Residents*, 112-3; *DSAB*, II, 212-3; Le Cordeur, *Politics of Eastern Cape Separatism*, 123-4, 144-5.

34 Philip, *British Residents*, 18; *DSAB*, I, 56-7; A.P. Buirski, 'The Barrys and the Overberg' (unpublished MA thesis, University of Stellenbosch, 1952); Edmund M. Burrow, *The Moodies of Melsetter* (Cape Town, Balkema, 1954), 91-85, 101-3; Edmund H. Burrows, *Overberg Outspan* (Cape Town, Maskew Miller, 1952), 229-76.

35 Philip, *British Residents*, 391; E.J. Inggs, 'Mfengu Beach Labour and Port Elizabeth Harbour Development, 1835-1870', *Contree*, 21 (1987), 5-12; A. Porter, 'John Owen Smith 1804-1871', *Looking Back*, XXIV (1984), 93-6, *Grahamstown Journal*, 7 May 1839, 4 November 1841.

36 *DSAB*, II; Burrow, *The Moodies*; Burrow, *Overberg Outspan*; Muller, 'Coastal Shipping', 12.

37 Philip, *British Residents*, 341-2; *DSAB*, II, 590-2; Muller, 'Coastal Shipping', 14-5; Theal, *Records*, IX, 311, XIV, 172; Cape Town, Government Archives P.C. 3/1.

38 D. Nash, *Bailie's Party of 1820 Settlers* (Cape Town, Balkema, 1982), 131-3; *DSAB*, II, 34-5; Shelagh O'B. Spencer, *British Settlers in Natal 1824-1857* (Pietermaritzburg, University of Natal Press, 1981), 5-9; *LAC*, II, 1964; Theal, *Records*, XIV, 33.

39 *DSAB*, II, 173-4; Eily H.A. Gledhill, 'William Cock, a Pioneer of Commerce', *Afrikana Notes and News*, XIV, 1960-1961, 83-7; Le Cordeur, *Politics of Eastern Cape Separatism*, 51, 89; *LAC*, II, 1826-1840, 123-8.

40 Gledhill, 'William Cock', 84, 86; Le Cordeur, *Politics of Eastern Cape Separatism*, 131, 196-7, 218, 259, 261-3; Eric W. Turpin, *Basket Work Harbour : the Story of the Kowie* (Cape Town, Timmins, 1964); *LAC*, II (1964); *DSAB*, II, 173-4; G.D.R. Dods, 'Nineteenth-Century Communications in the Zuurveld' (unpublished MSc thesis, Rhodes University, 1960), *passim*.

41 Philip, *British Residents*, 377; Cape Town, Government Archives, P.C. 3/1.

42 Morse Jones, *Roll*, 138; *LAC*, II, 1826-1840, 24.

43 *DSAB*, II, 488-9; Morse Jones, *Roll*, 143; *LAC*, II, 1826-1840; Cape Town, Government Archives, Colonial Office, C.O. 285, Remarks on the Navigation of the Kowie, 19 February 1826.

44 Nash, *Bailie's Party*, 134; *LAC*, II, 1806-1825, 28.

45 Philip, *British Residents*, 443-4.

46 Philip, *British Residents*, 52-3; Cape Town, Government Archives, B.O. 235, Private Diary of James Callander, Conservator of Forests, Knysna; Patricia Storrar, *Portrait of Plettenberg Bay* (Cape Town, Purnell, 1978), 40-1; Winifred Tapson, *Timber and Tides* (Cape Town, Juta, 1961), 2-4.

47 *DSAB*, III, 364.

48 Philip, *British Residents*, 145, 166, 218, 289, 325-6, 401.

49 Morse Jones, *Roll*, 140; Cape Town, Government Archives, C.O. 285, Port Frances, 1826; *Grahamstown Journal*, 26 June 1833, 25 February 1836.

50 Cape Town, Cape Town Government Archives, C.O. 285, Port Frances, 1826.

51 Nash, *Bailie's Party*, 134.

52 A.L. Muller, 'Some Questions about Port Elizabeth's Earliest Entrepreneurs', *Looking Back*, 22 (1982), 12-3; A. Porter, 'Port Elizabeth's First Trading Centre', *Looking Back*, 23 (1982), 62-4; A. Porter, 'Toll of the Sea; Shipwrecks in Algoa Bay', *Looking Back*, 23 (1982), 121-5; Theal, *Records*, XIII, 398-411, XXII, 386; Philip, *British Residents*, 40, 129-30.

53 Theal, *Records*, XXIII, 85-7.

54 London, PRO, C.O. 48, 107, f. 176; Theal, *Records*, 272; Marcus Arkin, *Storm in a Teacup : The Cape Colonists and the English East India Company* (Cape Town, Struik, 1973), 68.

55 Theal, *Records*, XII, 475; Cape Town, Government Archives, P.C. 1.

56 Cape of Good Hope, *Government Gazette*, 1825 and 1829.

57 Burrows, *Overberg Outspan*, 233-7; Cape Town, Government Archives, P.C. 3/1; C.O. 6099.

58 South African Public Library, Cape Town, MSC 9, George Rex's Ledger, 1817-1823, ff. 55, 76, 130, 176; Una Long, *An Index to Authors of Unofficial, Privately-Owned Manuscripts Relating to the History of South Africa* (Cape Town, University of Cape Town, 1947), 119, 158-60; Muller, 'Coastal Shipping', 14-5; Tapson, *Timber and Tides*, 3-4; Sanni Metelerkamp, *George Rex of Knysna* (Cape Town, Timmins, 1951), 102-21; Cape Town, Government Archives, P.C. 3/1; C.O. 6099.

59 Eric J. Inggs, 'Liverpool of the Cape: Port Elizabeth Harbour Development, 1820-1870' (unpublished MA thesis, Rhodes University, 1986).

60 *LAC*, I, 1802-1825 (1968), 38, 68, 69; *LAC*, II, 1826-1840, 3; Theal, *Records*, XVII, 31.

61 *LAC*, II, 1826-1840, 3; Theal, *Records*, XXV, 479, 272, XXX, 33; London, PRO, C.O. 148, 135, f. 116.

62 Margaret D. Nash, 'John Bailie at the Mouth of the Buffalo River', *Africana Notes and News*, XXIII, 1979; Keith P.T. Tankard, 'East London, the Creation and Development of a Frontier Community, 1835-1873' (unpublished MA thesis, Rhodes University, 1985), 64-7, 90-3.

THE P & O IN WAR AND SLUMP, 1914-1932:
THE CHAIRMANSHIP OF LORD INCHCAPE

Stephanie Jones

This paper, drawing on material analysed during research for a biography of the first Earl of Inchcape,[1] is part of a continuing discussion, in two respects. First, it concludes the account – begun in volume 17 of the *Exeter Papers in Economic History* – of the career of James Lyle Mackay.[2] The focus on that occasion was on Mackay as an overseas entrepreneur, one of a wave of Scots venturing out to new commercial frontiers including the Indian sub-continent, and seeking their fortunes there in the last quarter of the nineteenth century.[3] Here, we look at the last two decades of Inchcape's long life – he died in 1932 aged 80 – when he had risen to the leadership of one of the largest shipping combines in the world.

Secondly – and of wider interest – the paper continues the debate raised at the 1988 Dartington conference by Professors Helge Nordvik and Lewis Fischer (their paper will appear in the next volume of the conference papers) of the role of Norwegian shipping within the context of the world shipping industry in the inter-war years. They describe and analyse the comparative success of Norway in this period, in stark contrast with Britain's failure to adapt to new conditions and respond to new challenges. This study of Inchcape's chairmanship of the P & O suggests some further reasons why Britain was so relatively uncompetitive.

Introduction

The popular view of the P & O in Inchcape's day was one of a prestigious, prosperous and wealthy shipping line, of world-leading class. This was clearly indicated by one of the humorous maritime postcards shown in David Williams' presentation at the Dartington conference of October 1988.[4] But this joke – of a lady passenger borrowing a penny from a White Star Line steward who is insisting 'I want it back, this isn't the P & O!' – has a distinctly hollow ring to it. This present paper shows – through a basically chronological approach to the problem of the P & O's performance throughout the war years and the 1920s – that Inchcape's decisions were not always in the best interests of the long-term future of the P & O, and that he failed to confront the problems faced by British shipping as a whole in the inter-war years.

Inchcape's management of the P & O in the period 1914-1932 is fundamentally an account of how he maximised its income – including substantial transfers from his own personal wealth derived from the Mackinnon Mackenzie partnership and elsewhere – and maintained its interests, so that it could survive a dramatic fall in profitability and equally dramatic rise in costs after the First World War. This process of cash injections and financial manipulation cushioned the P & O – particularly its shareholders – from real losses and severe liquidity crises. A sustained and thorough attempt to put the P & O on a sound financial footing and establish efficient management was delayed until after Inchcape's death in 1932.

The Early War Years

The war accelerated Inchcape's already fast-growing public and political prominence, and his leverage in both the shipping industry and government circles reached a new height, to the extent that both he and the P & O were to emerge from the war stronger than ever. On the outbreak of war, the P & O benefited from an increase in income from government hiring and the rise in freights, earning a revenue for 1914 of nearly £5 million (hereafter m) and a profit of over £750,000, with reserves of £2m.[5]

Inchcape showed considerable dexterity in overcoming the immediate difficulties of the early war years. There was, initially, a problem of his own: the reluctance of P & O shareholders to acccept him as a replacement for the long-respected Sir Thomas Sutherland. The war was turned to Inchcape's advantage: it was, he argued to fellow-directors, no time for leadership disputes.[6] Instead, he emphasised the importance of patriotism and maintaining morale. He effusively congratulated P & O and BI captains who survived attacks of shelling, and forwarded to the Press descriptions highlighting the bravery of all ranks. He was especially concerned with relieving the anxiety of the large number of lascars – Asian seamen – employed by the group, who in some cases had taken fright and abandoned their vessels, leaving passengers to work the ships. At the same time, he drew attention to the P & O's extensive investments in war bonds and government securities, which were to total more than £16m by the end of the war.[7]

Another problem never entirely solved during the hostilities was the shortage of ships suffered by the P & O, caused by an increasing demand by the government for troopships and transports, and exacerbated by heavy casualties. Financial losses were partly offset by Inchcape's success in lobbying the government into accepting war risk insurance,[8] but he still had to replace the ships, and shipbuilders found it difficult to keep pace with demand. Inchcape was able to keep the vital mail service going through three strategies, adopted in 1915. First, he maintained sailings – and profits – by co-operating with other shipping lines. Inchcape arranged for the pooling of tonnage between the BI, the French Messageries Maritimes and British Union Castle, whereby each accepted each others' passenger tickets to make the best of the irregular services between Europe and East Africa. He also chartered vessels from the Indo-China Steam Navigation Company through Jardine Matheson in Hong Kong.[9]

Secondly, Inchcape ensured the future supply of newly-built tonnage through the powerful position he had established with the shipbuilding community,

132

particularly Alexander Stephen on the Clyde.[10]   In November 1915 he reserved the next two yard numbers, at a time when pressure on the yards was great.   He obtained this favoured treatment through his prestige and prominence in British shipping, and thus the need to cultivate his custom for the future.   And thirdly, Inchcape made up for the lack of shipping by maximising the earnings of vessels still at his disposal and not apparently required by the government.   He devised a series of special new tours, such as a £90 per head excursion for the many who generally wintered outside Britain, but who now found Continental resorts increasingly unattractive and dangerous.   The itinerary of this tour covered three months, including first-class accommodation from Marseilles to Bombay by mail steamer, connecting to a first-class rail service across India and back via Egypt.[11]

This third strategy may appear somewhat unpatriotic on the part of Inchcape and the wealthy and leisured passengers involved, but he felt it was important to emphasise a policy of 'business as usual' at the P & O, and it helped maintain the share price when other lines were suffering crises of confidence.   P & O deferred stock had reached £295 in 1915,[12] much higher than that of the Royal Mail Group, for example, whose results had been relatively disappointing.[13]   Despite their reservations, P & O directors and shareholders were now beginning to see the advantages of the merger between the P & O and the BI, and Inchcape's chairmanship.   1915 revenues were even higher than 1914 – over £5m – but the dividend on the deferred stock was maintained at 15 per cent in order to make provision for the uncertain future.   Inchcape appeared confident at the AGM, proudly drawing attention to the P & O's record of carrying 2.5 million men (not including 320,000 wounded), 1 million horses and 2.5 million tons of stores, with only 0.1 per cent loss of life.[14]

Inchcape's confidence was justified.   To colleagues at Mackinnon Mackenzie in Calcutta – the merchant partnership who acted as agents for the BI and with whom Inchcape had spent the first twenty years of his business career – he wrote: 'as you are aware, our [i.e. Mackinnon Mackenzie's] earnings during the last year have been abnormally large ... we have made enormously large profits'.   The BI had remitted home more than £1.4m from Calcutta in 1914, and payments were continuing.   It was more than enough to pay for new ships for both the BI and the P & O.[15]

This may be seen as the commencement of a process whereby Mackinnon Mackenzie, the BI, and other subsidiary and associated businesses were employed by Inchcape in financially supporting the P & O, which mainly came into effect after wartime profits had dried up in the 1920s.   Inchcape took the opportunity of the success of his first year in office to claim the same level of emoluments enjoyed by Sir Thomas Sutherland in the past: 2.5 per cent of the net earnings of the shipping line.   This assured his personal income and provided another source of funds for the P & O in the future.[16]

Inchcape sought a long-term solution to the P & O problem of a shortage of tonnage, and contributed substantially to the shipping line's power and prestige with a dazzling series of major acquisitions. He showed a skill in selecting targets and in negotiating deals inherited by his grandson in the expansion of the Inchcape Group in the 1960s and 1970s. The first new addition to the P & O fold came in 1916 with the merger with the New Zealand and Federal lines. In 1914-15, the ships of these fleets carried more than 75 per cent of all sheep carcasses carried by sea from New Zealand to the UK, and more than 50 per cent of the increased 1915-16 total. The earnings of the New Zealand and Federal companies – who owned 31 fine steamers of an aggregate 240,000 tons, only seven and a half years old on average – exceeded £1.4m in 1916. Seen as one of Inchcape's greatest bargains, the New Zealand and Federal lines were purchased with BI and Mackinnon Mackenzie cash and P & O paper for just £2.5m. These fleets were of immediate value in the mid-war situation and throughout the rest of Inchcape's chairmanship, and were to make increasingly large contributions to the P & O coffers.[17]

In 1917, Inchcape was to add a further 113 vessels to the P & O group fleet, a net gain of 96 ships in view of the P & O's loss of 9 and BI's loss of 8 ships in this year. These additions were the result of the acquisition of the Union Steamship Company of New Zealand, the Hain Steamship Company, the Nourse Line and the Mercantile Steamship Company.[18] As with New Zealand and Federal, these purchases were instantly valuable, and were to prove themselves even more worthwile in the future: the Union Company, for example, was to pay over £100,000 per year to the P & O by 1918, and regular 'special bonuses' reached over £1m in the late 1920s.

Fairplay and other shipping journals commented favourably on the wisdom of Inchcape's purchases, but not everyone shared their views. There were particularly strong objections in the Antipodean newspapers who, noting the sale of Australasia's 'most national concern' – a shipping line ranking seventh in the carrying trade of the British Empire – complained: 'is it expected that New Zealand will lightly stand aside and see this great concern wrested from our hands and pass into the control of a company which employs lascars, coolies and Chinese in manning its ships?'[19]

Suppression of the Accounts

Such opposition was of relatively little consequence to Inchcape, who was now consolidating his position as the unchallengeable leader of this expanding shipping combine. In order to set aside wartime earnings for future use without shareholder pressure to raise the dividend, Inchcape used the wartime situation to justify suppressing detailed information usually given in the P & O Report and Accounts, on the grounds that it was not desirable that this information should be freely available to the P & O's competitors at home and overseas. He could also argue that it was impolitic to maintain a high dividend in wartime, and would dissuade the Government from providing generous freights for hired vessels. Keeping all published financial details to a minimum became, after the war, a convenient device whereby Inchcape concealed the true picture of the group's economic position. The financial press described the new Report and Accounts as 'a very meagre document as compared with the old statements sent in under the Sutherland regime. There are no details whatever of operating charges'.[20] There was speculation of an inadequate allocation to depreciation, when previously this had been allowed for on a liberal scale. Doubts were generally silenced in view of the high share price: the deferred stock closed the year 1917 at £351.[21]

Post-War Government Compensation

In 1914, the BI owned 131 steamers of 598,203 tons, and the P & O comprised 70 larger vessels, totalling 548,564 tons. Purchases during the war years totalled 107 ships of 370,000 tons, and helped offset wartime losses of 66 ships, of over 440,000 gross tons aggregate. This loss, without the new acquisitions, would have been much more severe, and it was turned into a gain for the group, as Inchcape used his leverage at the Ministry of Shipping to extract the maximum compensation from the authorities. These lost vessels had originally cost nearly £8.3m in total when acquired; but their depreciated value by their date of loss was a fraction of this, estimated at only £3.7m, and they had been written down in the P & O books to only £1.8m. Inchcape, through determined bargaining in each individual case, won over £12m in compensation. The BI did particularly well: for 23 lost ships originally costing £2.2m, written down to just over £0.5m, Inchcape received £4m.[22]

Inchcape's best deal was undoubtedly the *Ballarat*. Lost in 1917, this 11,120-ton liner had cost £176,000 new five years previously, and was written down on the books to only £15,000. On approaching Sir Joseph Maclay, head of the Ministry of Shipping, Inchcape was told that the maximum compensation payable on this ship was £395,000. Inchcape argued with Maclay and his officials for over an hour, insisting on £420,000 and no less. He then announced, 'I will retire into the next room and smoke a cigarette and leave you to talk the matter over among yourselves.' Within ten minutes, they called him back and Maclay humbly declared, 'Lord Inchcape, you have been extremely useful and helpful to this Ministry all through the War. No words of mine can express the gratitude we feel. I am convinced you would not ask more for your ship than you consider you are entitled to get and we have decided to pay you £420,000.' In describing this incident later, Inchcape exclaimed, 'I think I did a fairly good hour's work for the P & O in getting this extra £25,000, and I drove back to the City feeling rather pleased with myself.'[23]

Few were in as strong a position as Inchcape to strike such a bargain. Inchcape's public work in this crucial period reached such a magnitude that he received a glowing acccolade in *The Times*: 'probably no civilian outside the

Cabinet discharged during the War a greater range of administrative activities'.[24] His work was regarded as so important that, as indicated in his comments above, he was one of the few private individuals awarded a petrol allowance for his motor car.

Post-War Strategy and Tactics

With the cessation of hostilities and the need to prepare for the post-war future, Inchcape reviewed the group's strengths. The P & O and BI were expected to resume their ascendancy in the Indian Ocean and Far Eastern trades - lost largely to the Japanese – and flex their newly-acquired muscles in Australasia. Mackinnon Mackenzie would further the group's interests as agents: the partnership's healthy profits – approaching nearly £1m per year – were mostly derived from P & O and BI commissions, and could be repaid in rebates when necessary.[25]

Yet instead of looking forwards, Inchcape looked backwards, by a process of temporary make-do-and-mend rather than future planning. His goal was largely to return to pre-war conditions which, understandably, he regarded as the norm. He saw a situation where Britain had lost 38 per cent of pre-1914 tonnage – more than every other combatant except Norway – and was now threatened in a number of traditional trades and markets, by new competitors and a decline in demand for tonnage.

Inchcape's short-term strategy was primarily concerned with maintaining the dividend, keeping the share price buoyant, and ensuring high shareholder morale. His tactics were a masterpiece of financial manipulation which achieved this aim, but at the cost of hiding a deepening crisis. The exact nature of the P & O group's financial position was revealed only after Inchcape's death in 1932, by an investigation instigated by his successor, Alexander Shaw, carried out by leading accountants Deloitte's.[26]

Deloitte's report described a powerful group, with large and important subsidiaries and associated companies owning half a million tons of shipping offering extensive services all over the Indian Ocean and the Far East. Yet its fleets were written down far too conservatively for a major undertaking in the financial conditions of 1932 – to only £14m – and the whole group was desperately illiquid. Provision for current and maturing liabilities was inadequate, and there was insufficient working capital, much of the reserves having been spent on new tonnage.

Table 1 shows that the 'net results' – the final figure revealed to shareholders – was totally unrelated to the earnings of the P & O fleet itself, revealed by Deloitte's investigations. These annual amounts are meaningless, as they were not related to earnings and disbursements occurring from year to year. Without their knowledge, shareholders' dividends were derived from contributions from subsidiaries and from members of the Mackinnon/Inchcape group – including Inchcape's private money in forsaken income – and from liberal allocations made from war-time profits.

TABLE 1

P & O 'Net Results' Compared with Profit Calculated by Deloitte's

(By taking into account depreciation at 5 per cent on cost, and by excluding special credits and dividends and bonuses from subsidiaries, Deloitte's presented the real picture of the P & O in the 1920s)

Year	'Net Result'	Carried over	Dividends Pref. Def.		Deloitte's adjusted
	£	£	per cent	per cent	£
1922	696,600	101,700	5	12	125,506
1923	1,013,200	101,800	5	12	1,017,244
1924	1,346,900	101,000	5	12	137,003
1925	1,273,500	142,100	5	10	345,141
1926	1,196,000	133,000	5	10	-306,237 loss
1927	1,200,000	118,000	5	10	513,591
1928	1,200,000	121,000	5	12	371,437
1929	1,200,000	120,000	5	12	-105,847 loss
1930	1,165,000	115,000	5	10	916,730
1931	947,800	115,000	5	6	-830,817 loss
TOTALS : £11,309,971					£2,183,751

Source : National Maritime Museum, P & O/12/8

Officially, the P & O made aggregate profits of £11m in the years 1922-1931, on which total dividends of £9.3m were paid out. According to Deloitte's, actual profits generated by the P & O totalled only £2.2m. £9.4m was contributed from sources outside the P & O itself, and from funds which should have been used for depreciation. Over this period, charges for depreciation would have exceeded £34m if calculated at the usual rate of 5 per cent per year on original cost: these charges were never allowed for.

Where did the funds come from to offset real losses, pay the P & O dividend, and enable Inchcape to maintain the deception of apparently inflated profits? The sources were many and varied:

- a special reserve fund set up during the war, £2m
- a contingency fund, also dating back to before 1918, £1.5m
- an insurance fund set up in 1914, £2.5m
- amounts recovered from Excess Profits Duties, totalling £1.6m
- a loan from merchant bankers Cohen, Laming and Hoare, £3.2m
- a loan from the P & O Bank, £2.9m
- 'special bonuses' transferred from the Union SS Co., £5.3m
- 'special bonuses' transferred from the NZ SS Co., £1.8m
- transfer from P & O employees' savings scheme, £1.4m
- Treasury grant to all shipping lines to offset obsolescence, £2.5m and, providing undetermined amounts:
- savings on insurance by insuring the group ships through Gray Dawes, another of Inchcape's partnerships, and reinsuring them on the open market
- rebates from Mackinnon Mackenzie, Gray Dawes and other members of the Mackinnon/Inchcape group.

The siphoning-off of cash from these funds – which totalled £24.9m – masked the fact that for the greater part of the post-war period, P & O group earnings were falling dramatically, and there was an especially severe decrease in gross receipts from passenger voyages. In 1929, the P & O fleet of 450,000 tons struggled to earn £7m gross, which 360,000 tons earned in 1922, and during 1923-6, earnings constantly fell below this point. After the temporary recovery of 1929, by 1931 gross receipts dipped as low as £5.8m. This was actually much worse than it appeared, as for the first time it also included earnings from the Branch line which provided services to Malta, Port Said, Suez, Aden, Colombo and Australia. Despite an annual mail subsidy of £300,000, the P & O found it could no longer provide a fortnightly service to Calcutta at a profit.[27] Deloitte's figures show year by year the amount that the P & O was actually generating, setting aside minimal depreciation allowances. What happened in these years to reduce earnings so much?

In the immediate post-war years, the group found itself facing increasing competition from Scandinavia, the USA and Japan. Inchcape's media 'Shipping and Shipbuilding Crusade'[28] drew attention to the predicament, but offered few solutions. It was especially critical of the Government's reluctance to release ships from war-related duties before 1922, at a time when there was an increasing demand for passenger services.

The short post-war boom detracted from many post-war problems, including that of the heavy increase in shipbuilding prices, competition from oil-fired vessels, and increasing labour unrest. By 1921, voyage profits had fallen to one-third of the previous year, although twice as many round trips had been performed. 1922 and 1923 were the last years in which P & O ships more or less broke even, due to the Treasury grant, a cut in wages, and income from trooping.[29]

1924, when government work came to an end, was the worst year on record, and Inchcape was forced to cut the dividend. Aware of the severity of the slump in shipping, the Government introduced the Trade Facilities Acts, which were to prove instrumental in giving Kylsant's Royal Mail Group an artificial lease of life; Inchcape did not see these subsidies as an answer to the fact that by 1926, of 172 voyages undertaken by his ships, only 36 made a profit. The General Strike added to the P & O's problems, leaving ships to sail without cargoes and resulting in a long-term rise in coal prices.

1927 was a better year, with a rise in the P & O share price at rumours of a merger with Cunard. The group spent heavily on a new turbo-electric ship, the *Viceroy of India*, a necessary decision if it was to continue to compete in the prestigious passenger trades. 1928 was better still, with losses of only half of those of 1927 and, after an extensive economy drive with heavy cuts in wages, Inchcape decided to restore the dividend. Thereafter, the group plunged into deepening crisis, as the subsidiary and associated services – which had provided much of the group's income in the past – also began to lose heavily, as a result of increased operating costs and strong local competition in Indian and Australian waters.

Inchcape's policy of manipulation and conservative finance effectively kept the group going during his chairmanship, but with the real sources of the P & O income rapidly drying up, this policy could not have been maintained for long. A contemporary observer within the P & O maintained that the revolution in the P & O's finances introduced by Shaw was long overdue, and that the group was on the verge of bankruptcy.[30]

Three particular features of the Inchcape administration were now singled out as especially responsible for the difficulties it now laboured under: the secrecy surrounding the accounts, the continued payment of generous dividends, and the failure to allow for depreciation.[31] The juggling of funds behind the scenes was replaced by detailed published information, so that shareholders and City commentators could see exactly what was happening. The dividend was immediately suspended and was not restored for several years. The allowance for depreciation and for fleet renewal and replacement was seen as of first priority.

Shaw inherited a shipping line suffering from the problems of British shipping as a whole, problems which Inchcape did little to offset. Competing nations, especially those newly developing their own national merchant fleets, took large chunks of Britain's markets and carrying trade, assisted by subsidies, tariffs and lower operating costs, whilst British ships remained largely unassisted by the Government until the mid-1930s. British exports fell sharply whilst imports rose, destroying tramp profitability and hitting the liner trade hard, especially with the parallel decline in emigration.

Why was Britain the only country besides Germany to experience a net tonnage decrease in the period 1914-1938, whilst the United States tonnage quadrupled, Japanese tonnage trebled and the fleets of Norway, Italy and Greece expanded by at least 100 per cent?[32] These competitors were comparatively small in 1914, and had enjoyed and maximised many opportunities for growth. But this does not explain why the British mercantile marine failed to match this growth.

There are basically four reasons why Inchcape's policies – among those of fellow British shipbuilders – did relatively little to improve matters. There are signs, however, that although in each case he was prepared to make changes, these were implemented all too slowly.

First, the structure of British shipping was strictly divided into tramps, liners and tankers, whilst foreign shipping companies were much more flexible and often owned all three types. The P & O was strictly a liner company, but with Hain and Nourse, Inchcape showed he was willing to diversify into tramping, and these vessels were more successful than many other tramp fleets in this period.

Secondly, British ships remained largely of the traditional pre-war type, without adequate appreciation of technical change; although Inchcape's final ships, such as the turbo-electric *Viceroy of India*, *Strathnaver*, *Strathaird*, show signs of making the most of shipbuilding progress. British shipbuilding as a whole stagnated technologically through its reliance on conservative British shipowners for orders, and its failure to establish markets for its products overseas.

Thirdly, British shipping was hidebound by its adhesion to the conference system, which aimed at making trade secure and reliable for the benefit of the shipowners, without trying to break into new markets. Inchcape was a great supporter of shipping conferences and was always highly critical of those trading outside them.

Fourthly, British shipping in the 1920s did not take full advantage of the great new fuel of the post-war years: oil. If only the British fleet had had more oil-fired ships, and if only it had made greater headway in the oil-carrying trade, the picture drawn here could have looked radically different. Sturmey has commented that, 'if enough British owners had responded in this way no decline in the position of the British fleet in the inter-war years need have occurred.'[33] And these remarks are directed towards Inchcape, as the outstanding shipowner of this period.

In short, British shipping in the 1920s and 1930s was run predominantly by the older generation – who constantly harked back to the old pre-war days – not by the new shipping men of the kind emerging in Scandinavia, the United States and Japan. Inchcape's attitude and approach of make and mend, of keeping the P & O going from year to year, of a grudging and reluctant acceptance of major shifts in trade and technology, was typical of the majority of his fellow shipowners. This factor fundamentally underlies the reasons for the international realignment of world shipping in the inter-war years.

NOTES

1   Stephanie Jones, *Trade and Shipping : Lord Inchcape, 1852-1932* (Manchester, 1989).

2   Stephanie Jones, 'British Mercantile Enterprise Overseas in the Nineteenth Century : the Example of James Lyle Mackay, First Earl of Inchcape', in Stephen Fisher, ed., *Studies in British Privateering, Trading Enterprise and Seamen's Welfare, 1775-1900* (Exeter, 1987), 79-97.

3   *Ibid.*, 84, n.3. This point is further discussed in Stephanie Jones, *Two Centuries of Overseas Trading : The Origins and Growth of the Inchcape Group* (London, 1986), which superseded P.J. Griffiths, *A History of the Inchcape Group* (London, 1977).

4   Dartington Maritime History Conference, organised by the Department of Economic History, Exeter University, at Dartington Hall, 22-23 October 1988. Mr Williams' paper is printed in this collection, but the particular postcard is not one of those reproduced with it. General accounts of the history of the P & O include David Howarth and Stephen Howarth, *The Story of P & O* (London, 1986); P.J. Griffiths, 'History of P & O' (unpublished typescript, in Inchcape archives); Boyd Cable, *A Hundred Year History of P & O* (London, 1937); and David Divine, *These Splendid Ships* (London, 1960).

5   Reports and Accounts of the P & O, National Maritime Museum (NMM), P & O 6/20-22.

6   Board Minutes and Agendas of the P & O, NMM, P & O 1/118-9.

7   Chairman's Statement, 1914 , see Note 5 above, and correspondence in British India Steam Navigation Company records (described in R.J.B. Knight, *Guide to the Manuscripts in the National Maritime Museum*, Vol. 2 (London, 1980), 27-30, NMM, BIS/8/4, 1912-22.

8   Select Committee on Insurance of British Shipping in Time of War, British Parliamentary Papers (1914), LXX.

9   See Note 7.

10 The papers of Alexander Stephen are held in the Archives of the University of Glasgow, Adam Smith Building. See entry by Anthony Slaven in *The Dictionary of Scottish Business Biography* (Aberdeen, 1987-8), 240-2, under 'Shipbuilding and Marine Engineering'. Inchcape's relationship with Stephen was discussed at length by the author in a paper presented to a University of

Glasgow symposium, 'The Shipping World and Scotland', May 1987 (unpublished).

11 P & O Handbooks, 1913-1932, NMM, P & O 42/15-26.

12 P & O Stock Prices, 1912-1937, NMM, P & O 29/16.

13 Reported in *The Financier*, 29 April 1915. See Edwin Green and Michael Moss, *A Business of National Importance : The Royal Mail Shipping Group, 1902-1937* (London, 1982), Chap. 3, 21-40.

14 Chairman's Statement, 1915 AGM, NMM, P & O 6/20-23.

15 NMM, BIS/8/4 1912-1922.

16 Lord Inchcape's Remuneration, 1912-1925, NMM, P & O 12/6.

17 See Knight, *Guide to the Manuscripts*, 50-2; Stephanie Jones, 'Maritime Commerce in the Pacific from the Mid-Nineteenth Century to the 1920s : The P & O and Inchcape Companies', in Clark G. Reynolds, ed., *Global Crossroads and the American Seas* (Missoula, 1988), 171-80; John Maber, *North Star to Southern Cross* (Melbourne, 1967), 121-35; NMM, P & O 35/1, Booklet on New Zealand Shipping Co.; and Company Balance Sheets, NMM, NZ 4/4-12.

18 Amalgamation with the Union Company, NMM, P & O 31/2, 6; Mercantile, P & O 35/65; Hain, P & O 35/69-71; and Nourse, see Knight, *Guide to the Manuscripts*, 52-3.

19 *The British and Australian Times*, 16 August 1917.

20 *Financial Times*, 30 November 1915.

21 See Note 12.

22 Ships lost in World War I, NMM, P & O 101/14.

23 Quoted by Hector Bolitho, *James Lyle Mackay : First Earl of Inchcape* (London, 1936), 125.

24 *Ibid.*, 130.

25 Correspondence, 1912-1922, NMM, BIS/18/4.

26 Report by Deloitte's, NMM, P & O 12/8.

27 Results of Voyages, 1919-29, NMM, P & O 5/566.

28 Letter by Inchcape in *The Times*, reprinted in *Fairplay* (shipping journal), 24 October 1918.

29 These year-by-year analyses are based on P & O Annual Reports, Board Minutes and Voyage Accounts, as referenced above.

30 Wilfrid Mizen, who joined the P & O in 1913 and rose to become Company Secretary, for whose insights the author is most grateful.

31 First Chairman's Statement by Alexander Shaw, 1932, NMM, P & O 6/27.

32 See the discussion in H.J. Dyos and D.H. Aldcroft, *British Transport. An Economic Survey from the Seventeenth Century to the Twentieth* (Leicester, 1969), 343-55.

33 S.G. Sturmey, *British Shipping and World Competition* (London, 1962), Chap. IV.

AN ILLUSTRATED SOURCE FOR MARITIME HISTORY :
THE PICTURE POSTCARD, 1894-1930

David M. Williams

Anyone contemplating what medium represents the most extensive source of visual record of life in the early twentieth century in Europe, and for that matter the world, might well feel that the choice lies between illustrated books; film, especially early newsreels; and the press, newspapers and magazines. None of these choices would be correct, for, in fact, the greatest source of visual record is the postcard. To most observers, and certainly the vast majority of historians, such a statement must seem preposterous; the postcard appears as a trivial inconsequential item, one only occasionally resorted to, normally in fulfillment of the obligation to send holiday greetings! But, however understandable such a view, it reflects a total ignorance of the role and universality of the postcard during the opening decades of the twentieth century. In that period the postcard was an important element of popular culture and a pervasive feature of everyday life. Gaining an appreciation and the acceptance of these facts is not easy, and the present writer is under no illusion as to the extent of the credibility gap to be bridged. It is therefore necessary, before considering the value of the postcard as a historical source, in this instance in a maritime context, to demonstrate its remarkable popularity in the years from the turn of the century down to the early nineteen-twenties.

The postcard, in the form of a stamped pre-paid card issued by the Post Office was introduced in Britain in 1870. It was not, however, until October 1894 that the Post Office relaxed its monopoly and permitted the usage of privately published postcards bearing a picture. It is from this date that the picture postcard, as generally conceived, came into being.[1] From the outset, the new innovation proved enormously popular. Within nine years, in 1903, the Post Office was reported as handling over 600 million cards and, by 1910, the figure was estimated at over 800 million.[2] A clearer perspective of the implications of such figures is gained by relating them to the population; this produces a consumption figure of around twenty-five cards per head per year. But for every sender of a postcard there was also a receiver, so on average each individual, in terms of sending and receiving, was handling around fifty cards per year. Such statistical calculations, however, relate solely to cards which passed through the post. Many others did not. Some may have been delivered personally by hand to family and local friends; many more still were never passed on, but rather were purchased or acquired to keep as a casual memento or purposely to collect. Now, how many cards fell into these latter categories, and what was the ratio between cards purchased and cards consigned to the postal services, must be a matter for conjecture. But enquiries of leading dealers and auctioneers in the current postcard trade suggest that the ratio was certainly not less than 2 : 1, and may have been as high as 4 : 1.[3] Even drawing on the conservative estimate pushes up annual consumption per head to around 100 cards, and should one move to a consideration of household consumption then the figures take on quite remarkable proportions. Clearly in the Edwardian era, the postcard was very much a feature of everyday life.[4]

The postcard owed its great popularity to various reasons. It possessed enormous utility as a means of communication. It was cheap, postcards retailing at one penny or a half penny each, or less for multiples, while postal rates down to 1917 were a half penny inland and one penny overseas.[5] In an age when telephones were few, and personal transport the preserve of the rich, the card was ideal; and its limited message space could be regarded as a virtue. Again, at a time when few possessed cameras, the postcard could serve as a memento or souvenir, and it should be recognised that postcards were attractive items in their own right, especially when good photographic reproduction and colour printing in books and the press was not common. All these features appealed to a newly, more widely aware, more literate and more mobile population. Furthermore it must be said that in the Edwardian era postcards had a novelty appeal so that sending and collecting cards became very much the 'in thing', in fact a contemporary craze with clubs, competitions, mammoth collections, magazines and much else.[6] Of course nothing remains new for ever and there are indications that the novelty phase of the postcard was at its peak around 1910, but World War One served to sustain the popularity and usage of the card. The removal of the stimulus of great events combined with other changes – rising postal rates, wider use of the telephone, colour illustrated magazines, new media in the form of radio and cinema – all combined to diminish the special attributes of the postcard and to bring about a decline in its popularity. Cards continued to be produced in vast numbers and were still widely used, but to use the hackneyed phrase, the 'golden age' had passed.

In the heyday of the postcard, the great demand for postcards was facilitated and fuelled by developments in printing and publishing. New rotary presses and advances in colour printing raised production potential in both scale and quality and lowered unit costs. Postcard publishing became big business and many major national and international firms emerged.[7] But, because the costs of entry into the business were very low, small local enterprises could effectively compete and find their own niche in the market. Many local photographers, printers and stationers quickly recognised the commercial opportunity of the postcard. The potential was enormous as cards could be produced to suit every occasion, subject and sentiment. The variety of themes depicted on cards is infinite. There were view cards; art, children's, comic and greeting cards as well as cards depicting entertainment, patriotic themes, royalty, transport, politics, issues and events of the day. The list can be extended indefinitely and most items could be portrayed at local or national levels.[8]

As remarkable as the scale of postcard publishing and the variety of its product was the universality of the business. The postcard was international, being produced and used everywhere. Usage in Britain was limited compared with Germany and also lagged behind France and the United States.[9] Even more revealing of worldwide participation is the 1906 figure for postal usage in Japan, almost 500 million, in a country in the early stages of modernisation.[10] Clearly, the postcard met a common human need and served a worldwide clientele.

The phenomenon of the postcard is of interest to historians on two counts; as an element of social history in its own right and in the legacy of visual images which it has passed down. The legacy comprises those postcards which have survived, which given the card's fragile and ephemeral qualities, can be but a fraction of all those produced. Yet the quite staggering multi-billion numbers of cards issued and the widespread habit of collecting cards in family albums, subsequently retained for sentimental reasons, ensures that enough have escaped destruction to provide a rich source of visual record.[11]

For the maritime historian the postcard offers a variety of possibilities as a visual source, indeed one might say that postcards can be found depicting every aspect of sea-going craft and their settings, both in a British and an international context. Ship portraits, dock and harbour scenes, cargo handling, the fishing industry, unusual events, wrecks and disasters, launches and homecomings, naval personalities, and happenings in war and peace, almost everything deemed unusual, topical or of interest found its way on to the postcard. The above examples relate to real life scenes captured by the photographer, or, less frequently, created by the artist, and these represent the chief areas where the card has something to offer. But the postcard like any other form of graphic presentation could also be used to portray images, moods, and sentiments, sometimes with advertising or propaganda connotations, and this applied in the maritime field as much as any other.

In considering the utility of the postcard as a source for maritime historians, it is important to focus on those areas where the postcard provides material which is unavailable or less accessible elsewhere. To observe that the postcard offers splendid illustrations of ocean liners, battleships, naval life and personalities, and coastal architecture such as docks, lighthouses and piers, is certainly true, and the postcard may well provide a fresh angle or perspective, but in such areas visual material is available elsewhere and in abundance. Thus while not losing sight of the almost complete range of maritime subjects illustrated by postcards, this paper concentrates on identifying some areas where the card has a more original contribution to make. As examples it focuses on three aspects: first, as illustrative of the postcard's utility as a straightforward visual image of maritime activity, it considers illustrations of vessels and located incidents and events, both the mundane everyday scene and the unusual; secondly, as an indication of the postcard's historical significance in its own right, it examines shipping company advertising; and thirdly, as an example of how the postcard can convey an impression of attitudes, it looks at the image of the sailor's lot, and popular views and propaganda in World War One. Finally, having indicated some of the opportunities presented by the postcard, a concluding section discusses the validity and usage of the medium.

The most obvious example of the maritime history postcard is the card which portrays a vessel, usually named or identified. Whereas cards depicting named sailing vessels are relatively uncommon, it is probably true to say that most steam powered vessels of the opening decades of the century, mercantile and naval, were at some stage in their careers depicted on the ubiquitous postcard. Some postcard publishers specialised in ship portraits; C.R. Hoffman, who boasted the splendid address of No. 1, The Docks, Southampton, produced a lengthy series of liner studies, including some outstanding interiors, is perhaps the best example. Others included the Kingsway Company which specialised in real photo studies, and B. & A. Fielden of Blundellsands, Liverpool who were prolific publishers in the inter-war years. An indication of the scale of operation of such specialist publishers, and the market they served, can be gained from statements made by O.W. Hoffman, son of C.R. Hoffman, who was responsible for the diversification of his father's tobacconist business into postcards. He observed, that in the nineteen-thirties, in the Southampton docks area, he had six outlets, served by twenty girls, plus six boys with portable stands, offering 'today's ship postcards' at 'seven a shilling'. His remark that 'on a good day postcard sales could bring in £100' represents a one-day sales' figure of 14,000, a staggering number, revealing both a measure of the scale of the enterprise and the extent of popular demand.[12] Of course, ship portraits are an area of maritime history illustration which is not in short supply; there are vast collections held by a number of institutions, the National Maritime Museum's archive being the outstanding example. Yet, the ship postcard portrait, apart from sometimes providing a view from a different angle or in a uncommon setting, may also have something to offer in two distinctly different areas.

The first of these is that of the artist drawn ship portrait. Whilst the majority of ship cards comprised a photographic image, a not insubstantial number were art work of some quality. The firm of Raphael Tuck, doyen of postcard publishers and possessors of the Royal Warrant, produced a range of series – 'Celebrated Liners', 'Our Dreadnoughts', 'The British Navy', 'The Fleet in the Far East' and many others – all superb art studies.[13] In this instance the art work was largely unattributed but in most other cases the studies were signed, and by marine artists of some repute. Artists such as James Spurling, the Blacks – Algernon and Montague B., Arthur Burgess, Charles Dixon, James Mann, Kenneth Shoesmith, Walter Thomas, to name but a few of British origin, while famous continental ship artists included the Belgian impressionist Henrie Cassiers, E.I. Lessieux, Alfred Praga, Odin Rosenvinge, Willi Stower and Max Ullman. Some of these studies were painted specifically for postcards and thus are unique, others may have originally been produced for a larger format, perhaps posters for publicity (something to be considered later), but it is worth noting in this context that the postcard may have enjoyed a higher survival rate than some other forms of ephemeral material. And, lest the art study postcard be dismissed because of its relatively diminutive size, the excellence of colour printing in the opening decade or so of the century, sometimes chromo-lithography of an exquisite standard, permits an enlarged image of remarkable quality. The ship postcard art study thus has a not inconsiderable potential.

Of course it was natural for ship artists to concentrate on important vessels, mercantile or naval, in the public eye; but the further area where the postcard ship portrait has something to offer is at the other extreme, that of small craft, often merely of local significance. Vessels such as coasters, tug and pilot boats, fishing smacks, river and estuary steamers, pleasure boats, ferries – the very sort of vessel which is likely to be excluded from the major archive collections – are all to be found on the postcard. The wealth of material of this nature, which is not to be underestimated, emanates from the activities of local postcard producers. The business of postcard publishing was democratic in the sense that there was scope and opportunity for both large and small, national and local, publishers. The large national publisher, aiming for a wide circulation tended to be selective in his choice of subject; local publishers were more catholic, photographing and publishing anything which might have an appeal to their immediate clientele, or in a resort context, the tourist or casual visitor. Hence the photographing of the humble vessel for which the postcard may be the only record.

It is appropriate at this point to comment on the role of the local photographer in the first twenty years of the century. At that time the ownership of cameras was limited to a very few; moreover, local papers were likely to be entirely unillustrated other than for the line drawing sometimes to be found in the advertising section. Thus the local photographer performed a dual function, that of serving the photographic needs of individuals and families, taking portraits, groups, weddings etc. but also that of recording the setting, social life and memorable incidents in the experience of the community. The latter would be printed in limited runs for local sales.[14] All settlements, from the small town upward, were capable of supporting at least one locally-based photographer. In Cornwall, local photographer-publishers included Argall, Gibson, A.H. Hawke and E.A. Bragg, the last named well known for his magnificent studies of Cornish shipwrecks; active in a similar field were the Scilly Island family firms of Gibson and King,[15] and prominent amongst Devon photographers were Chapman, Montague Cooper, Dyer, Gay, Knight and Twiss Bros. Such West Country names must serve as exemplars for the whole of Britain, though such photographers as Sutcliffe of Whitby, Sankey of Barrow in Furness, and Harvey Barton of Gloucester and South Wales, are sufficiently well known for their maritime studies to justify a special mention.[16]

The small photographer-publishers portfolio was actually a wide one; local vessels, local scenes, harbour views, dock activity and the fishing industry were all part of his staple fare, and were photographed again and again from different perspectives, often over a number of years. Such a pictorial record is of enormous value to the historian, with background detail often as rewarding as the foreground images. Even more fascinating may be the product of the local photographer's practice of recording anything of an unusual or out of the ordinary nature. Thus the postcard provides illustrations of such things as storm damage, wrecks, lifeboats and their crews, and parades, processions, gatherings of one kind or another – anything impinging on, or involving, the community. Unless the photographer's original material has survived, the postcard may be the only repository of this local visual record.

The consideration of the postcard as a record of maritime activity has drawn its examples from the British context. However, this should not be taken to imply anything special or unique about the postcard in Britain. Without doubt the British postcard heritage is very great, but no richer than that of other western European countries and certainly inferior to that of France. But even a European focus might be seriously faulted as too narrow, for one of the postcard's greatest virtues is its universality. Postcards were to be found all over the world, even in the remotest parts, and in its pictures of native craft, isolated ports of call, primitive cargo handling and the contrast between the new and the centuries old, the postcard may have an even more vital role as a visual source.

Besides representing a record of history, the postcard may also be an element of history in itself. In a sense, the postcard like any other contemporary printed material or dated artefact is of the past and therefore part of history. However, the point to be stressed is that the postcard, besides providing a visual representation of the past, may at the same time convey an indication of contemporary attitudes or practice. Thus the material produced by local photographers/publishers, particularly relating to special events, nor merely illustrates contemporary life but is indicative of the strength of community interest and feeling which provided the market for such products. Perhaps the distinction being made here between the record and element of history is best shown by an example; a straightforward ship portrait of the *Titanic* is simply an item of record, but an 'In Memoriam' card produced for sale after the disaster is a piece of history in itself, as it conveys the enormous contemporary impact and sense of loss, quite beyond present day comprehension. And if in our example the memoriam card, in terms of design was multiplied forty-fold and more – as was the case – then the significance of the postcard as history is immensely reinforced. It must be said, regrettably, that the example just quoted – and the flood of similar cards associated with the Hull trawler outrage of 1906, the *Lusitania* and the *Gladiator* disasters – bears out the adages of 'profit from adversity', and from a publicity standpoint 'no news like bad news', but there are less harrowing examples indicative of the postcard as history. One such is the use by shipping companies of the postcard for advertising purposes.[17]

Advertising and merchant shipping have a long relationship as a glance at the commercial page of any early newspaper clearly shows. Press notices of vessels preparing and loading for departure to a given destination, often with a small design indicative of a shipping advertisement, are apparent from the mid-eighteenth century. Over time however the nature of shipping advertising changed, developing by the late nineteenth century, to one in which the visual image became more, and ultimately, all important. Underlying this shift were a variety of factors: the development of an advertising industry itself,[18] the pioneering and refinement of the poster as a publicity instrument,[19] tremendous advances in printing, and within the business of shipping a growing orientation towards passenger traffic. The market in which all shipping companies were operating was increasingly competitive. At a local level, coastal freighting carriers were faced with inland railway services; more recently established steamer and excursion services were competing in the recreation and holiday market, and in ferry services to British islands and the Continent, railway companies were the bitterest rivals. In all these contexts shipping companies resorted to advertising. Above all, liner companies did so. As restrictive, conference-type agreements controlled frequency of sailing and limited price competition, so shipping lines competed in services; advertising provided important publicity.

In the main, in the period from the late nineteenth century to the 1940s, shipping companies advertised through graphic art presentation, utilising the media of poster, postcard, brochure and booklet. The postcard was widely used by business generally in the opening decades of the century as cards were familiar to, and popular with, the public; could be kept as a souvenir, and had a message-bearing utility.[20] Shipping companies appreciated that their postcards were especially attractive in each of these ways, moreover they had long provided headed stationery to meet the seemingly irresistible desire of all passengers to inform friends of their voyage. Postcards, visually more pleasing and easier and briefer to use, had an enormous advertising potential for shipping companies. In themselves, then, such postcards are actual advertising instruments; they also depict the wider spectrum of shipping company advertising. This is because the same designs were widely used for cards, posters and other publicity items. This duplication of images is very fortunate, because advertising material, being ephemeral, has a high destruction rate. The postcard has survived better than many other forms, in particular, the poster. The record of many shipping poster designs resides solely in their postcard reproduction.

The level and quality of advertising by shipping companies varied, being related to resources and circumstance. Short-distance freight and excursion companies advertised as best they might, according to needs and resources. In the main, however, shipping advertising focused on the larger shipping lines. In this area, advertising was on a massive scale reflecting the crucial importance attached to it, the funds available and the intensity of the market place. Liner company advertising became highly sophisticated involving the advertising agencies, commissioned artists and utilising the latest in printing and design. Such attention was paid to advertising because companies were seeking not merely to inform but also to establish a company image of quality, high-standard service with the emphasis on style and luxury. Hence artwork was preferred to the camera; ship portraits combined both grace and power; shipboard scenes showed a glamorous lifestyle; exotic locations en route were depicted, and posters were bold and striking, often innovative in what was a new art form and in keeping with first, the 'nouveau', and then the 'deco' style.[21]

Given the scale of shipping advertising, and the number of companies and artists involved, a full listing is beyond the scope of this paper. Confining a list only to British shipping companies which issued cards would exceed 120 entries without taking account of the many railway companies with shipping interests.[22] Even so, a few names deserve mention on the grounds of the volume and quality of material produced. Leading companies included the Allan Line of Canada; Canadian Pacific; Cunard;[23] the French Line, CGT; Hamburg-Amerika; Maritime Belge du Congo, CIE; Messageries Maritimes of France; NYK of Japan; Norddeutscher Lloyd; P & O; Red Star Line; Royal Mail; Union Castle, and White Star. That so many of these were involved on the trans-Atlantic is indicative of that route's preeminence and the ensuing high level of competition. Amongst the many artists involved in producing studies for advertising purposes especially outstanding were Odin Rosenvinge who did work for the Cunard, Allan and the Anchor Lines; Charles Dixon for the Red and White Star and Holland-Amerika; Montague Black and Walter Thomas, both for the White Star; Bernard Church and James S. Mann, both for Cunard; Henri Cassiers, a long-standing artist with Red Star; Frank Mason for Cunard, Holland-Amerika and the coasting Everard Line; Ernest Hamilton for Elder Dempster and Ellerman; Kenneth Shoesmith, a prolific designer for Cunard and the Royal Mail Steam Packet Line; and J. Spurling, highly regarded as a marine artist, particularly for his sailing ship studies, who did much work for P & O. Within this galaxy of talent, Dixon, Rosenvinge, Shoesmith and Cassiers were outstanding, with the latter enjoying a reputation within, and far beyond, the maritime sphere.[24]

Although by its very title the picture postcard is primarily the presenter of a visual image, it can also serve as an indicator of attitudes, mood and sentiment. In a sense the cards discussed in the context of 'visual images' and 'the card as history', while serving these functions, simultaneously say something about attitudes. They all certainly reflect an interest in things maritime and in many cases an intense fascination with local and national events. Moreover, those concerned with disasters, especially the spectacular, or those which touched on Britain's honour or prestige as a nation, reveal an enormous emotional association and commitment. In the main however all the types of cards referred to so far, with the exception perhaps of a few advertising items, have been cards which photographically or artistically provided a straightforward representation of a maritime scene – a vessel, harbour scene, personalities and so on. But besides these essentially real-life images there were other types of card which had a maritime theme. Artistic impressions of sea and ships, greetings cards which drew on maritime images, historic studies portraying past naval glories, heroes and famous vessels, and humorous cards depicting sailors and the seafaring life. All these serve to demonstrate the importance of the sea and all things connected with it within the popular culture. As an example of how cards, which are not illustrations of real life yet which nevertheless have significance for maritime historians, this section examines two maritime themes widely portrayed in the comic postcards of the period 1900-20, namely the image of the sailor and the naval experience of World War One.

The comic postcard of the early twentieth century has a poor legacy in the form of seaside cards and the coarse obscenities of the present day.[25] Down to the early 1920s, comic cards were generally witty representations of the human condition and circumstance and, though quality varied, were often the work of commercial artists of considerable repute. Moreover, because comic cards had a general appeal and were aimed at a mass market, they were largely the preserve of major publishing companies and produced in very long print runs.[26] The seaman was a stock figure of the period. For identification purposes he was always shown in naval uniform, or at least cap and bell-bottoms. Aboard ship the seaman was portrayed as fit, eager and enthusiastic; ashore, the setting most favoured by artists, he was invariably depicted as being in pursuit of a 'good time'. Wine and women, with just an occasional song, were the inevitable ingredients. All this is entirely predictable, what is less so is that the seaman could be shown in situations of excess. Sailors were pictured not just enjoying a drink but rowdily drunk, worse for wear, or 'hung over'. Again, while the sailor might be innocently portrayed in company with females, he was far more likely to be shown less purely motivated. He was to be found appreciatively ogling pretty faces, neat ankles and the contemporary 'Gibson Girl' hour-glass figure; or seeking ladies of the town or accosting serving girls – while abroad, in pursuit of the same, nudity and colour went by the board. Jokes about conceptions coinciding with shore leaves, and seamen receiving surprise bundles when they returned to port were not infrequent, while the seaman's response to religion, or the worthy efforts of individuals and institutions concerned with his welfare, was portrayed as indifferent, ungrateful or cynical.

All these images of the sailor were conveyed in a humorous style, sometimes witty, often rough and ready, occasionally a shade crudely – whichever, the point to be stressed is that the seaman's behaviour was not being held up to condemnation, rather, it was being viewed with a measure of tolerance. This is quite remarkable given that all the images quoted were in contradiction of contemporary attitudes on drink, morals, sex and religion and flouted the prevailing code of what was decent and respectable. Clearly an exception was being made in the case of the seaman: such latitude was not afforded to other sections of the labour force, not even soldiers or policemen, and significantly comic artists did not portray other workers in a similar vein. Thus the comic image emphasises, albeit in an unusual manner, some of the complex elements which shaped society's ambivalent attitude to seamen, namely a recognition of his unique position and the special affection he was accorded.

Postcard portrayals of the sailor, particularly his excesses ashore, were of course no more than traditional images depicted in a new medium. Eighteenth- and nineteenth-century cartoons and prints tell the same story. Events in 1914, however, represented a sharp break with the past, and the unprecedented new experiences and circumstance of war provided fresh themes and images for all branches of the media. The volume of postcards with a maritime connection produced during the war was enormous; perhaps surprisingly so, given that the navy's participation in the war did not assume quite the role which had been envisaged for it. The long awaited heroic engagement of the Grand Fleets never fully materialised, and for Britain the struggle at sea increasingly became one of protecting supply lines and combatting the submarine menace. Comic postcards reflected both initial hopes and subsequent reality. The outbreak of war gave rise to a flood of images evoking the spirit of Nelson and Trafalgar, fully confident of a speedy, decisive and glorious outcome. This soon gave way to frustration and contempt for a cowardly enemy fleet portrayed, to list only a few images, as a cornered rat, mouse in a hole, rapidly rusting or being overgrown by grass, and giving new meaning to the phrases 'corked' or 'bottled up'.

Yet for all the mass of cards castigating Germany's cautionary tactics, there were more on the theme of U-boats and the counter measures taken against them.

Torpedo, U-boat, zig-zagging, convoy and blockade all became part of the common vocabulary. To see hundreds of images on these aspects is to appreciate how far the anti-submarine campaign impinged on public consciousness and culture. The favoured imagery of U-boat/torpedo theme jokes, that of children in baths, or drunks in horse troughs or fountains, or arriving home to face marital wrath and censure, may seem banal, but when seen in their totality these cards represent a measure of mass awareness and involvement to supplement the evidence of more conventional sources.[27] Nor should the morale boosting impact of such mocking of adversity be ignored: the portraying of real danger in absurd, laughable situations is an accepted psychological defence mechanism and an established propaganda technique. But the comic postcards referred to were not government inspired propaganda – far from it – they were the product of profit-seeking publishers, producing for a commercial market. Such entrepreneurs were publishing material which they believed reflected the public mood and would therefore readily sell. The implications of this bear not merely on all the comic maritime cards of World War One, but on all the postcards of the pre- and post-war eras and indeed virtually all cards at all times. The postcard was the product of businessmen serving and exploiting a market; only if they thought an item was in accord with public demand, taste and sentiment, would they produce it.

The previous discussion has indicated a variety of ways in which the postcard can illustrate and inform in the field of maritime history. It is hoped that many who might have been hitherto ignorant or dismissive of the postcard will now recognise its considerable potential. Even so, however successful this paper has been in its proselytising function, one suspects that a certain amount of scepticism may remain – embodied in the question, 'is this small, very humble medium really a significant source for maritime historians'? The answer is best given by posing another question, 'how important is the visual image to maritime historians'? There is nothing evasive about such a response, rather it serves to put the postcard into perspective. There can be no doubt that the visual image is highly significant: at its lowest level it colours, illustrates and gives life to material gained from manuscript and printed sources; at another level the visual may be evidence in itself confirming findings from elsewhere or serving as a source in its own right; and at arguably an even higher level, the contemporary visual image may be history in itself as much as any other artefact from an earlier time.

Hence, our original question, essentially, 'how important is the postcard' can be broken down into two questions, 'does the postcard possess these varied facets of the visual image' and 'how important is the postcard *vis à vis* other sources of visual image'? To the former the evidence of what has gone before must testify; on the latter, the opening statement of this paper can only be reiterated and amplified. For the first quarter, or perhaps the opening forty years, of the twentieth century, the postcard is the most abundant and universal of all visual sources. Local, national and international; embracing both photographic and art forms; its designs serving varied functions, and published both in terms of individual units and print run in numbers which strain credulity, the postcard in its versatility and generality had no equal.

The potential of the postcard is all the more because of the limited use made of the medium. Past usage of the postcard in general terms, not merely maritime cards, offers a strange and, in some ways, sad contrast. Professional, academic historians have drawn very little on the source.[28] This neglect stems from a general reluctance to use visual sources and from an ignorance of the specific medium of the postcard. Both these features are compounded by the problem of accessibility. In the main, libraries, record offices and museums have viewed postcards and other items of ephemera as outside their remit; and in many cases, beyond the pale and beneath their dignity. Hence the sort of collections and archives which academic historians are familiar with, and have access to, have not accumulated postcards. In fairness, it must be said that a few such institutions are now belatedly beginning to recognise the value of the postcard though it is now infinitely more difficult and costly to build up a postcard archive than, say, in the early 'sixties.

In contrast with academic historians, history enthusiasts and local publishers working on a narrower level and fired by either the local history or postcard collecting booms, have assembled private collections of cards through diligent hunting, local advertising and purchase at antique shops, fairs and auctions. Such accumulations have formed the basis for, over the past twenty years, a veritable flood of illustrated books – mostly topographical, town or county based, drawing heavily, and sometimes exclusively, on the postcard.[29] Many of these works are most interesting and their role in bringing old images to light and presenting them to a wider public is praiseworthy indeed. Some, with coastal locations have considerable maritime relevance. Yet the quality of such volumes is very mixed; a few are quite outstanding, but a high proportion are of the '.... as it was' or 'pictures of life in .... at the turn of the century' *genre*, while some, transparently honest, are simply entitled this or that place 'in old picture postcards'. Such publications are not without historical merit, but equally, it would be true to say that most offer, at best, a very superficial kind of history. For too many the medium is the message, the illustration is an end in itself, whereas it should be an element of a wider canvas of historical perspective. By not placing the illustration in a context built up from a whole range of historical sources, the story it can convey is left incomplete and an enormously rich opportunity is lost.

These general strictures on the use of the postcard apply perhaps less in the maritime field where usage, at a local or national level, or on a period or thematic basis, has been relatively limited. Coastal settlements have received less attention than industrial centres and market towns, and shipping, thankfully, has not yet suffered from the introvert fanaticism of so many train, tram and bus enthusiasts. The maritime postcard, until now spurned by professional historians and as yet little adulterated by common, nostalgic usage, has much to offer: in return, an informed utilisation of the source might gain for it a measure of the academic and serious recognition it deserves.[30]

All cards illustrated are slightly reduced in size. The standard dimension, universally adopted after 1902, was 5.5 x 3.5 inches. All the cards featured were of this size.

SHIP PORTRAITS
top. *City of Rochester*, photographic card by H.W. Herbert, Chatham; postally used (hereafter p.u.), 1911.
bottom. Dover pilot boat, real photo card by Charles Morris, Dover; Edwardian period.

SMALL PORTS AND HARBOURS
top. Polperro harbour, photographic card by Photochrom Co. Ltd, Tunbridge Wells; p.u. 1938 – clearly, much later than the date of the original photo.
bottom. Westbay, Bridport, real photo card by Hider, location unknown; no indication of date, probably 1920s.

WRECK AND DISASTER
top. The *Magdelene Tristan* wrecked on Chesil Beach, Portland, real photo card; publisher unnamed; date uncertain.
bottom. The *Herzogin Cecilie* ashore at Salcombe, April 1936, a real photo card, part of a series by A.E. Fairweather, Salcombe.

CASUALTIES AND SURVIVORS
top. Caister lifeboat *Beauchamp* and crew, real photo card by Papworth, location unknown, p.u. 1912.
bottom. The six survivors of the wreck of the *Hilda*, wrecked off Brittany, 19 November 1905. The majority of casualties were Breton onion sellers returning home after the selling season; collotype, one of the series by a French publisher HUM; date – contemporary with the tragedy.

EVENTS AND OCCASIONS
top. Multi-view card commemorating visit of Japanese Navy to Greenock to take delivery of the newly commissioned HIJMS *Katori*, May 1906. Photo print by H.W. Jones, 27 Nelson Street, Greenock.
bottom left. Souvenir/Advertising card for the *Success*, allegedly the last surviving Australian convict ship, which visited English ports as a tourist attraction 1905-6; b & w art study, no publisher; p.u. 1906.
bottom right. Nelson centenary commemorative endeavouring to combine Trafalgar celebrations with the new *Entente Cordiale*. Coloured art montage, signed W.F. Mitchell, by C.R. Moody & Co., Ryde; 1905.

THE *TITANIC*

top.   *Titanic* disaster commemorative, b & w unsigned art study, published by Valentine, Dundee.

bottom.   Very rare Danish *Titanic* commemorative featuring the ship's gallant orchestra and the poignant hymn "Nearer my God to Thee" played as the vessel was sinking; b & w printed card by N. Kirk, Aarhus.

SHIPPING COMPANY ADVERTISING – SMALLER OPERATORS

top.   Publicity card for Southampton, I. of W. South of England Royal Mail Steam Packet Company. Coloured art card issued by the Company; c. 1908.

bottom.   Publicity card for Cosens and Co's Pleasure Steamers serving ports in Hampshire, Dorset and Devon, I. of W. and France.   B & w printed card with coloured house flag, published for the Company by Sydenham's Library, Bournemouth; p.u. 1903.

SHIPPING COMPANY ADVERTISING – POSTER STYLE I

top left.   Publicity card for the Allan Line, coloured art card issued by the Company; c. 1906.

top right.   Publicity card for Empress Steamers, coloured art card issued by the Company; date uncertain.   A printed message on the reverse reads, 'One should enter the New Year as the emigrant enters the New World – Stout of heart.   These beautiful Empress boats of the Canadian Pacific have carried many folk to fortune. May the New Year do as much for you.' [!]

bottom left.   Publicity card for Companie des Messageries Maritimes, coloured art card issued by the Company's Geneva Agency; n.d. but Edwardian era.

bottom right.   Publicity card for W. Lindsay, travel agents, Edinburgh, navy & white card issued by the Company; p.u. 1910.

SHIPPING COMPANY ADVERTISING – POSTER STYLE II

top.   Publicity card for Cunard Line, coloured art card signed O. Rosenvinge issued by the Company; c. 1930s.

bottom.   Publicity card for Yeoward Line, coloured multi-view art card issued by the Company; c. 1920s.

SHIPPING COMPANY ADVERTISING – ART AND DESIGN

top.   Publicity card for Red Star Line, coloured art card, unsigned, but by H. Cassiers, issued by the Company; c. 1905.

bottom.   Publicity card for the Japanese N.Y.K. Line, coloured art card with photo vignette, issued by the Company; date uncertain but probably pre-1914.   The reverse of all the Company's cards carried the slogan, 'The sun never sets on the N.Y.K. flag.'

SHIPPING COMPANY ADVERTISING – GRACIOUS LIVING

top.   Publicity card for Royal Mail Steam Packet Company, coloured chromo-lithograph issued by the Company; c. 1904.

bottom. Publicity card for Navigazione Generale Italiana, coloured card issued by the Company; n.d. but c. 1920s.

IMAGES OF THE SEAMAN – I
top. Glossy coloured comic art card, unknown publisher; p.u. 1910.
bottom. Coloured comic art card, unknown publisher; p.u. 1911.

IMAGES OF THE SEAMAN – II
top left. Glossy coloured comic art card, published by 'National Series'; c. 1908.
top right. Coloured chromo-lithograph comic art card by Wildt & Kray; c. 1906.
bottom left. Coloured comic art card, signed Donald McGill, by Inter-Art Co., London; 1917.
bottom right. Coloured comic art card, signed Donald McGill, by Inter-Art Co., London; 1916. Note dual captions in English and French in the hope of war-time sales abroad.

WAR AT SEA – INACTION
top. Coloured comic art card, signed H.P. [Harry Parlane], by H.B. [Hutson Bros.], London; c.1916.
bottom left. Coloured comic art card, signed Donald McGill, by Inter-Art Co., London; 1915.
bottom right. Coloured comic art card by Valentine, Dundee; c. 1916.

WAR AT SEA – MINES AND SUBMARINES
top left. Coloured comic art card, signed Donald McGill, by Inter-Art Co., London; 1916.
top right. Coloured comic art card, signed D. Tempest, by Bamforth, Holmfirth; p.u. 1917.
bottom left. Coloured comic art card, signed Donald McGill, by Inter-Art Co., London; 1917.
bottom right. Coloured comic art card, signed T.R., by Edward Hamilton, London; c. 1916.

SHIP PORTRAITS

CITY OF ROCHESTER.

SMALL PORTS AND HARBOURS

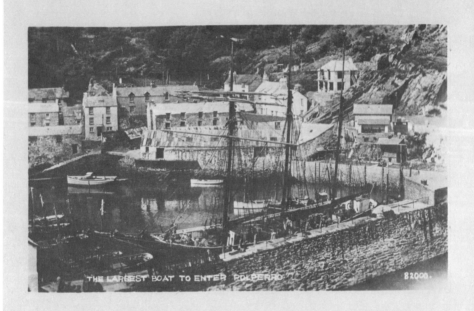

WRECK AND DISASTER

"Magdelane Tristan" Wrecked on Chesil Beach

HERZOGIN CECILIE ASHORE IN FOG AT SOAR MILL SALCOMBE APRIL 26/36. No 2.

CASUALTIES AND SURVIVORS

The Ill-fated Caister Lifeboat "Beauchamp"

Saint-Malo
Naufrage du "HILDA" (19 novembre 1905)
Les six survivants.

EVENTS AND OCCASIONS

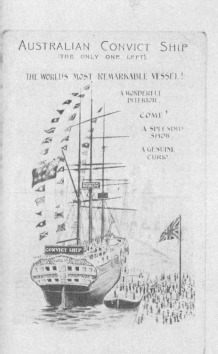

THE TITANIC

AMONG THE ICEBERGS

The Most Appalling Disaster in Maritime History.
The White Star Liner "TITANIC," sunk on her maiden voyage, off Cape Race, 15th April, 1912.

„Titanic"s Orkester,

der hin rædselsfulde Nat i April 1912 helte-
modig gik under med Kæmpeskibet, spillende
den kendte, engelske Salme: Nærmere, Gud,
til dig, (alt imens ca. 1600 Mennesker sam-
tidig fandt Døden i Bølgerne).

„Nærmere, Gud, til dig".

Nærmere, Gud, til dig,
  nærmere dig!
Er det end Korsets Vej,
  du viser mig,
allid dog synger jeg:
:,: nærmere, Gud, til dig, :,:
  nærmere dig!

Oplødt mit Øje ser
  Stigen til Gud,
og gennem alt, hvad sker,
  sendt paa dit Bud
Engle, som vinke mig
:,: nærmere, Gud, til dig, :,:
  nærmere dig!

Om sent i Sorgens Stund
  ensom jeg gaar,
og har til Leje kun
  Stenen saa haard,
Drømmen dog bærer mig
:,: nærmere, Gud, til dig, :,:
  nærmere dig!

Her er med Himlens Haab,
  Bethel for mig;
Stenen i Taarers Daab
  salver jeg dig.
Frejdig gaar frem min Vej
:,: nærmere, Gud, til dig, :,:
  nærmere dig!

Og er for sidste Gang
  Striden forbi,
Sjælen til Himmelvang
  løfter sig fri.
Evigt da jubler jeg
:,: hjemme, min Gud, hos dig, :,:
  hjemme hos dig.

SHIPPING COMPANY ADVERTISING
– SMALLER OPERATORS

SOUTHAMPTON I. of W
SOUTH of ENGLAND
ROYAL MAIL
STEAM PACKET COMP? LIMT?

SOUTHAMPTON

BRIGHTON

BOURNEMOUTH

ISLE OF WIGHT

S.S. LORNA DOONE

COMPANY'S FLEET OF PLEASURE STEAMERS
BALMORAL – LORNA DOONE – QUEEN
SOLENT QUEEN &C
Printed by E J Frampton Town Hall Avenue Bournemouth

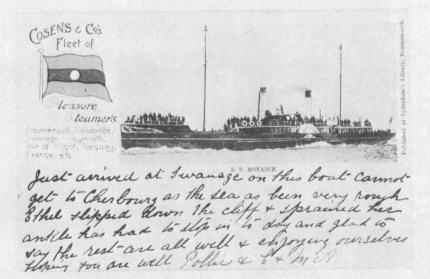

COSENS & Cºs
Fleet of

Pleasure
Steamers.

Bournemouth, Boscombe,
Swanage, Weymouth,
Isle of Wight, Torquay,
France, etc.

Published at Sydenham's Library, Bournemouth

S.S. MONARCH.

Just arrived at Swanage on this boat cannot get to Cherbourg as the sea as been very rough Ethel slipped down the cliff & sprained her ankle has had to stop in to day and glad to say the rest are all well & enjoying ourselves Hoping you are well Pollie & C & McR

SHIPPING COMPANY ADVERTISING
– POSTER STYLE I

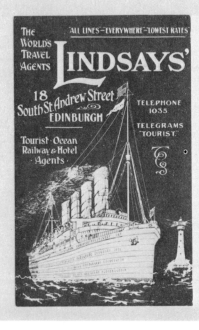

SHIPPING COMPANY ADVERTISING
– POSTER STYLE II

SHIPPING COMPANY ADVERTISING
– ART AND DESIGN

SHIPPING COMPANY ADVERTISING
– GRACIOUS LIVING

THE ROYAL MAIL
STEAM PACKET COMPANY
"R.M.S.P. AMAZON"

SOCIAL HALL

AVGVSTVS.

IL PONTE
DEGLI
SPORTS

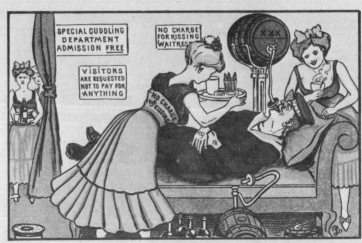

A DREAM OF HEAVEN

IMAGES OF THE SEAMAN II

Jack Ashore.

THEY ALL LOVE JACK.

JACK DETAILED FOR SCOUTING.

"Do you save women as well as men, Guv'nor?"
"Verily, brother — oh verily."
"Well, save one for me, will yer?"

"Please, can you tell me the way to 'Agnes
Weston's Home'?"
"No, matey; I can't—but I can tell yer where
little Katie Korfdrop lives!"
"Pouvez-vous me dire où est le 'Foyer du
Soldat'?"
"Non, mais je peux t'indiquer une maison
où tu ne t'ennuieras pas!"

WAR AT SEA – INACTION

WAR AT SEA
– MINES AND SUBMARINES

The Sailor's Dream.
"The sea, the sea, the open sea!"

Le Reve du Marin:
La liberte des Mers!

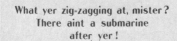

What yer zig-zagging at, mister?
There aint a submarine
after yer!

I TO U :

U FAST U BEAT U BOATS
U FEAST U BOATS BEAT U !!

1   Frank Staff, *The Picture Postcard and its Origins* (Lutterworth, 1966).

2   Statistics of postal usage are taken from Richard Carline, *Pictures in the Post* (Gordon Fraser, 1959), 39.

3   Over many years, I have received enormous assistance from members of the postcard collecting trade. In particular, I am grateful to Ken Lawson, proprietor of Specialised Postcard Auctions, Cirencester, and long-standing leading dealers Ron Mead, Ken Stubbs and Joan Venman. All have given freely of their time and expertise.

4   Good general studies of the picture postcard and its social impact are Carline, *Pictures in the Post*; Tonie and Valmai Holt, *Picture Postcards of the Golden Age* (MacGibbon and Kee, 1971); Frank Staff, *Picture Postcards and Travel* (Lutterworth, 1979). Also of value is A.W. Coysh, comp., *Dictionary of Picture Postcards* (Antique Collectors Club, 1984).

5   Postcards were very cheap, mostly one penny or a half-penny or cheaper, sometimes literally ten a penny. Moreover many cards were free, being given away for advertising purposes.

6   Features of the postcard craze were postcard clubs; specialist magazines; albums, blotters and wallets for use with postcards; competitions where winners sometimes amassed over 20,000 cards; and even the publication of numbered, limited edition portfolios of cards for investment purposes! An interesting contemporary handbook is W.J. Scott, *All About Postcards* (1903).

7   Anthony Byatt, *Picture Postcards and their Publishers* (Golden Age Postcards, Malvern, 1978).

8   An indication of the huge range of themes and subjects covered by picture postcards can be gained from the following picture postcard catalogues: *Picton's Catalogue*, eleven editions (BPH Publications and Longmans, 1971-84); *RF Catalogue*, three editions (RF Publications, 1985-7); *Stanley Gibbons Catalogue*, four editions (Stanley Gibbons Publications, 1981-5).

9   In terms of topographical and social history cards, France probably enjoys the richest postcard heritage. The *Neudin Catalogue*, published annually since 1975, and infinitely more detailed than British catalogues, contains extensive listings on a departmental, city, town and village basis.

10   See Carline, *Pictures in the Post*, 39.

11   Such was the popularity and ubiquity of the postcard that almost all households possessed family albums in the Edwardian era. It was this accumulation of cards in albums, and their subsequent retention for reasons of personal association and sentiment, that accounts for the survival of so many cards.

12   *Picture Postcard Monthly*, No. 109 (May, 1988).

13   On the firm of Tuck see Byatt, *Picture Postcards*, 287-301; Sally S. Carver, *The American Postcard Guide to Tuck* (Carver Cards, Brookline, Mass., 1976), and a regular monthly column in *Picture Postcard Monthly* since March 1980.

14   On the activities of local photographers see Martin Parr and Jack Stasiak, *The Actual Boot : The Photographic Postcard Boom 1900-20* (A.H. Jolly/ National Museum of Photography, 1976), and Byatt, *Picture Postcards, passim.*

15   *Picture Postcard Monthly*, No. 47 (March, 1983); No. 90 (October, 1986).

16   A list of significant local postcard publishers, compiled on a county basis, is to be found in the 1982 edition of *Picton's Catalogue.*

17   David M. Williams, 'A New Medium for Advertising : the Postcard, 1890-1920' *European Journal of Marketing*, 22, No. 8 (1988), 17-34.

18   D. Hindley and G. Hindley, *Advertising in Victorian England 1837-1901* (Wayland, 1972).

19   Max Gallo, *The Poster in History* (New American Library/Hamlyn, 1975).

20   See Williams, 'A New Medium', 34, for a list of major companies utilising postcards for advertising.

21   Bevis Hillier, *Histoire de l'Affiche* (Librairie Fayard, Paris, 1969-70).

22   A comprehensive listing of shipping companies which engaged in advertising is to be found in the 1987 edition of the *IPM Catalogue.* The list was compiled by Tom Stanley, to whom I am indebted for information on shipping companies, publishers and artists.

23   Philip Rentall, *Historic Cunard Liners* (Atlantic Transport Publishers, 1985). This work draws heavily on postcards and includes advertising material.

24   On Henri Cassiers and Red Star Line advertising see, *Picture Postcard Monthly*, No. 65 (September, 1984); No. 67 (November, 1984).

25 F. Alderson, *The Comic Postcard in English Life* (David and Charles, 1969).

26 In the period 1914-18 comic postcard publishing was dominated by three companies: the International Art Co.; J. Bamforth & Co.; and the Art and Humour Publishing Co. All three operated on a massive scale and employed the leading comic artists of the day, notably Donald McGill, Dan Tempest and Frederick Spurgeon.

27 Children, drunks and domineering wives were all members of the repertoire of stock comic characters. The impact of new and very real dangers was lessened by the use of such standard, familiar images.

28 A rare example of academic usage is that of J. Richards and E.J. Evans, *A Social History of Britain in Postcards 1870-1930* (Longman, 1980) though its excessive concentration on topographical/real life illustration inhibits a full appreciation of the complete range of postcard imagery.

29 A list of all books of topographical interest using postcards as illustrative source material published in the past decade would run to hundreds of entries. Merely as examples of studies with a maritime interest see Robin Fenner, *Devon and Cornwall Illustrated* (Stannery Press, 1986); Michael Rouse, *The Coastal Resorts of East Anglia* (Terence Dalton Ltd., 1982). Thematic studies are far fewer, but worthy of special mention are Hugh McKnight, *Waterways Postcards 1900-1930* (Shepperton Swann, 1983) and a quite marvellous presentation of World War One cards, Tony and Valmai Holt, *Till the Boys Come Home* (Macdonald and Jane's, 1977).

30 I am indebted to my colleague Dr P.L. Cottrell for his comments on an earlier draft of this paper.

Notes on Contributors

K.H. Hamilton-Smith is a practising naval architect, and has an interest in ships of the classical period.

E.C.B. Corlett is a naval architect and engineer, who has published extensively on nineteenth-century iron and steam ships, and the history of European catamarans.

Basil Greenhill is a former Director of the National Maritime Museum, Greenwich, a Hon. Research Fellow of the University of Exeter and a Co-Director of the University's New Maritime History of Devon project. He has published extensively on the history of nineteenth-century shipping and the archaeology of boats and ships.

Andrew Lambert is a Senior Lecturer in Strategic Studies at the Royal Military Academy, Sandhurst, and has a number of publications on British naval administration and policy in the nineteenth century.

Alison Grant is Chairman of the North Devon Maritime Museum, Appledore and a member of the Steering Committee of the New Maritime History of Devon project at Exeter University. She has published a number of works on North Devon's maritime history.

E.A.G. Clark is an Associate Professor in the Institute of Education at Rhodes University, Grahamstown, South Africa. In the maritime field he has published on the history of the Exe estuary, its ports and shipping, as well as other subjects.

Stephanie Jones, currently in the business world, is a former Historian to the Inchcape Group. She has published a number of works on the group's history and on British shipbuilding among other subjects.

David M. Williams is a Lecturer in Economic History at the University of Leicester. He has published widely on British nineteenth-century maritime affairs, particularly to do with Liverpool, free trade and seamen's conditions.

Stephen Fisher is a Co-Director both of the newly-established Centre for Maritime Historical Studies at the University of Exeter, and of the University's New Maritime History of Devon project. He has a number of publications in British and Portuguese commercial and maritime history.